HISTORY OF THE WORLD
VOLUME III

IMPORTANT DATES AND EVENTS

1000 B.C. Phoenicians build Carthage and explore coast of Italy.

800-700 B.C. Six farming villages unite to become the city of Rome.

750 B.C. Cumae, first Greek colony in Italy, settled by refugees.

509 B.C. Romans drive out the last of the Etruscan kings.

353 B.C. Rome expands, conquering the towns of nearby Latium.

312 B.C. Work begins on Appian Way, first Roman road.

280-256 B.C. Rome fights a Greek army under Pyrrhus, wins control of entire Italian peninsula.

264-146 B.C. Rome and Carthage at war.

218 B.C. Carthaginian army under Hannibal crosses the Alps to invade Italy.

204 B.C. The Roman general, Scipio, invades Africa, menaces Carthage.

203 B.C. Hannibal, recalled from Italy, meets Scipio in battle of Zama and is defeated.

196 B.C. Deaths of Hannibal, Scipio.

146 B.C. After nearly three years of siege, Roman troops capture Carthage, enslave its citizens, and burn the city to the ground.

IN ROMAN HISTORY, 1000 B.C.-44 B.C.

133 B.C. Tiberius Gracchus elected tribune, murdered by Senate.

124 B.C. His brother Caius Gracchus elected, passes many reform laws.

121 B.C. The mob turns on Caius and forces him to commit suicide.

107-86 B.C. Struggle for power between Marius and Sulla, which ends only with the death of Marius.

73-71 B.C. Slaves, led by Spartacus, revolt; they are suppressed after two years of fighting.

60 B.C. Pompey, Julius Caesar and Crassus form the First Triumvirate to combat the power of the Senate.

58-50 B.C. Caesar, commander of the legions in Gaul, subdues the barbarians; Pompey plots in Rome.

49 B.C. Caesar crosses the Rubicon with his legions; Pompey and the Senate flee; Pompey is crushed at the battle of Pharsalus.

48-46 B.C. Caesar, charmed by Cleopatra, stays in Egypt.

46 B.C. Caesar returns to Rome, begins to consolidate his power and enact reforms.

44 B.C. Caesar assassinated by Cassius, Brutus and other Senators. Civil War breaks out.

HISTORY OF

Editor Irwin Shapiro

Associate Editor Jonathan Bartlett

Consultant Albert Fried,
Department of History,
Queens College, New York

Contributors Anne Howard Bailey
John Bowman
Ormonde de Kay, Jr.
Edith Firoozi
Albert Fried
Johanna Johnston
Ira N. Klein
Willis Lindquist
Edna Ritchie
Seymour Reit
James L. Steffensen

VOLUME III

THE UNIVERSAL
THE WORLD

ANCIENT ROME

by James L. Steffensen

GOLDEN PRESS NEW YORK

CONTENTS

DESIGNED AND PRODUCED BY ARTISTS AND WRITERS PRESS, INC. PRINTED IN THE U.S.A. BY WESTERN PRINTING AND LITHOGRAPHING COMPANY. PUBLISHED BY GOLDEN PRESS, INC., NEW YORK.

The City of Aeneas

1000 B.C. - 500 B.C.

THE minstrels who wandered from country to country in the ancient world told a legend of Aeneas, a Trojan prince. According to the story, Aeneas escaped the Greeks who broke through the walls of Troy and fled to his ships with a little band of warriors. Rowing out onto the Hellespont, they watched while a great fire destroyed their city, and they knew that they could never return to Troy. Then, the storytellers said, the gods spoke to Aeneas, telling him to turn his ships west. They commanded him to sail away from the Hellespont and the Aegean Sea, past Crete and the country of the Greeks, into the unknown western ocean. There he would find a new land and build a new Troy, a mighty city that would conquer the Greeks and all the world.

Aeneas obeyed the gods and sailed west. But before he came to the place where his new city would be built, he knew many years of adventure and hardship. A storm wrecked his ships on the coast of Africa, where he was found by Dido, the queen of a great city called Carthage. Dido took Aeneas to her palace and told her people to greet him like a prince. And, while he lived in the palace, waiting for new ships to be built, the queen fell in love with him. She begged him to give up his wandering and his dream of a new Troy. She would make him king of Carthage, if only he would stay with her. When he refused, she killed herself, calling on the gods to grant her curse: "May Carthage and the city of Aeneas be enemies, make war on one another, and live in hatred forever."

But Aeneas sailed on, until he came to Italy

and the ancient Greek city of Cumae. Here, the minstrels said, he met the Sibyl, a mysterious and powerful priestess who could speak with the gods. She told him how to find the site which the gods had chosen for his city. Then she gave him a book in which was written the future of the city for more than 800 years, and the names of its heroes and enemies. Aeneas turned north, traveling by land, and at last came to a mountain that stood above a green, hilly plain and a river. And there, as the gods had promised, he found good land, and he began to build a city. This city was called Rome, and it became the great city of the West and the conqueror of the world.

Years later, in the time of the Caesars, when the Roman Empire surrounded the Mediterranean Sea, generations of minstrels had told the story of Aeneas countless times. The Romans liked to believe that it was true. It seemed only right that so great a city should have been founded by a prince and planned by the gods. And, indeed, many things in the story were actual history. There had been a Carthage and a Cumae. It was also true that a band of sea-warriors had come to Italy from Asia Minor, from a place perhaps not far from Troy. But the storytellers had forgotten

DIDO CURSED THE SHIPS OF AENEAS.

that this did not happen until long after the Trojan War.

The true story of Rome began somewhere around 1,000 B.C., when Phoenician sailors first ventured into the unknown western half of the Mediterranean Sea. Sailors from Crete and the first Greek cities already knew the eastern Mediterranean as well as they knew the streets of their own towns. But their world stopped at the island of Sicily. The rest was a mystery—dangerous, and too far away to matter.

TRADERS AND PIRATES

The Phoenicians were merchant-pirates, who had good reasons to look for havens in out-of-the-way places. They built the city of Carthage on the coast of North Africa, and from there, they went exploring along the coasts of the western part of the Mediterranean. It was rough, uncivilized country, but the hills were rich with metals—gold, silver, iron for weapons, and even tin. Tin was still so rare that it was used for jewelry and for decorating the palaces of kings. Near Carthage itself, the ocean floor held great beds of the shellfish whose ink was made into Tyrian Purple, the most fashionable and expensive dye in the ancient world. The Phoenicians found that trading was just as profitable as piracy. They hauled their western goods to the wealthy cities in the East, and Carthage became rich and powerful.

In the true story of Rome, it was the sailors from Carthage who first explored the west coast of Italy. Trading in the ports of Greece and Egypt, they began to tell stories about the green peninsula northwest of Greece. They called it Vitelliu, which meant "calf-land." a country of cattle and rich fields. When the Greeks heard these stories, they believed that they were just sailors' tales. Their own explorers had scouted the east coast of the same peninsula, and they said it was all mountains, with no good fields or harbors. In any case, like the seas beyond it, it was too far away to matter.

Then the eastern world was attacked by barbarians. It was not the first time that this had happened, for Europe, to the north, was filled with restless, warring tribesmen. The huge continent seethed like a great cauldron. And, from time to time, the cauldron boiled over, spilling its angry people over the rim of mountains that usually kept them from the Mediterranean lands. About 1000 B.C., Europe boiled up as never before, and horn-helmeted savages poured into Greece. For two hundred years they came, burning the towns and driving the Greeks from their fields. Homeless Greeks fled across the Aegean to look for new homes on the islands or along the Asian coast. But there was never enough land for all of them, and always the invaders were at their heels. Some of the refugees remembered the tales about Vitelliu and decided to sail west.

This time the Greeks went to the far side of the peninsula, the western side that faced away from the world they had always known. There they found the green fields and good harbors that the Carthaginian sailors had told them about. The mountains which the first Greek explorers had seen were only on the eastern side. When the news reached Greece, one shipload of colonists after another set off for Vitelliu, though their scouts warned them that winning land there would not be easy. Other men had heard of the rich peninsula, too, they said. Some of them had already settled there—the barbarians, the Carthaginians, and a third group of settlers who were called the Etruscans. Colonists from Greece would somehow have to come to terms with all three.

When the Greeks landed, they found the plains dotted with the farms and little huts of the barbaric tribesmen. The barbarians had been the first settlers to arrive in Vitelliu, at about the same time that their kinsmen had invaded Greece. They had come south through the Alps, struggling over the steep wall of mountains which guarded the northern end of the peninsula. Like their kinsmen, who had driven the Greeks from their homeland, the tribesmen were fierce fighters. But they could not hold back the Greeks who came to Vitelliu. These Greeks were well-organized, well-armed, and determined to win a foothold in the new land. They took turns standing guard, building walls, and clearing fields. As their settlements grew, they welcomed as citizens any of the barbarians who were willing to live with them in peace, and fought off those who were not.

The Greek colonists did their best to get along with the Carthaginians. At first, this usually meant staying out of their way. Carthage's own tough colonists had settled on all the islands near Vitelliu—on Sicily, just off the southern tip of the peninsula; and on Corsica and Sardinia, to the west. But they had left the mainland to the savages, because they wanted seaports and mines, not fields for raising cattle. When the Greeks turned up, the Carthaginians did little to interfere with them and even began to trade with them. All was well, so long as the Greeks kept to the mainland. After a few years, however, the Greeks began to set up colonies on Sicily. The Carthaginians protested angrily, but the Greeks went on building. The island became the home of two sets of rival cities, Greek and Carthaginian, which lived side by side in an uneasy peace because neither was strong enough to destroy the other.

The Greeks were much more cautious in dealing with the third group of settlers. These were the people called Etruscans, because their strongholds were in Etruria, the widest of the plains in the center of the peninsula. They were a nation of sea-warriors with a powerful fleet and strong armies. A hundred years before the first Greek colonists came to Vitelliu, a squadron of Etruscan war-boats had suddenly appeared in the channel between the peninsula and Sicily, and had pushed their way past the Carthaginian ships which guarded the passage. The warriors sailed up the coast, took the land they wanted, and held it with their spears. Like Aeneas in the legend, they had come from Asia Minor. They were not Trojans, of course. But when they landed in Etruria, in their bright plumed helmets and jangling metal jewelry, they brought the civilization of the East to the West, and the building of cities in Vitelliu began. By the time the Greeks arrived, the Etruscan settlements were so strong that the new colonists did not dare to go near them. The Greeks built their towns on the southern tip of the peninsula, well away from Etruria, and avoided the Etruscans except when they came to trade.

For two hundred years or more, the four very different peoples shared the riches of Vitelliu, and life on the peninsula began to change. Olive trees and grapevines were planted. And, as the plants took hold in the new land, so did many other things of the eastern world. In the south, the Greek cities grew and prospered. But it was in the center of the peninsula, the area of the Etruscans, that the first great changes came about.

The Etruscans were builders as well as warriors. They dug tunnels and built dams to drain the

ROME BEGAN AS SIX FARMING VILLAGES.

marshy fields, and they put up houses of sun-baked bricks. Their twelve city-kingdoms in Etruria had paved streets and were protected by heavy walls. The Etruscans taught the barbarians the secret of using wedge-shaped stones to build arches of great strength. And they began to pronounce the name of the land in a new way—now, and for thousands of years to come, it would be Italia. In English, it would be known as Italy.

LIFE OF THE ETRUSCANS

For the barbaric tribesmen, who would one day be the Italians, the Etruscans were conquerors, teachers, and often a puzzling mystery. When the tribesmen camped in the hills above the new towns, they heard for the first time the sound of flutes and the strange, throbbing music of Asian songs. They saw men whose everyday clothes were as brightly colored as their metal armor was strong. Later, as the tribesmen were defeated in battle or came of their own accord to live in the cities, they became the subjects of Etruscan masters. They learned to play the Asian music themselves. They threw away the animal skins they had worn and put on *togas,* flowing folds of cloth the Etruscans wrapped themselves in. On festival days, they joined the singing and dancing that sometimes went on all night.

From their new masters, the Italians learned to love everything that made life pleasant and gay—music and games, the bright colors they wore, wall paintings in their houses and temples. When trading—and sometimes piracy—made the Etruscans rich, they filled their homes with fine Greek pottery and decked themselves with jewelry of silver and gold. Life was to be enjoyed, they said, because death was a time of agony. They frightened the barbarians with stories and pictures of demons who tortured the spirits of the dead. And they taught them to celebrate funerals of important men with duels. The demons would torture the ghosts of the men sacrificed in the duels and leave the other spirits in peace.

Like all seafarers, the Etruscans worried about the gods who controlled nature—the winds and the sun and the seasons. They saw omens of good or evil in every lightning flash and shooting star. Before they planted crops or went to battle, their priests tried to foretell what would happen by studying the livers of sacrificed animals. Many of the omens must have been good, for the Etruscan warriors went to war often. For nearly 300 years, armies from the cities in Etruria won victories all along the peninsula—from the great Po Valley under the Alps to the plains and foothills of the southwest. They captured dozens of little Italian towns, among them the busy market town that would be called Rome. Then they marched far to the south, to the walls of the Greek cities. And there they stopped.

The Greek colonists in Italy had had time to put up good defenses, and now they could call for the help of the Greek settlers on the island of Sicily. The Etruscans had only their own troops and their Italian subjects, who deserted them as soon as war with the Greeks began. Cities the Etruscans themselves had built suddenly locked their gates against them. Then a new wave of barbarians battled through the Alps and attacked from the north. Slowly the Etruscan armies, squeezed between the Greeks and the barbarians, retreated into Etruria. In their own cities they were safe. But never again did they put on their

THE ETRUSCANS ENJOYED DANCING AND MUSIC IN THEIR FRESCOED HOUSES.

helmets and march in triumph through Italy.

The victorious Greeks did not conquer the peninsula—at least, not with weapons. But now it was their turn to be the teachers of Italy. From their cities in the south, their ideas spread along the peninsula and conquered it for all time.

Like Aeneas in the story, the Italians found wisdom in Cumae and the other Greek settlements. Again, when the storytellers told it, they mixed up the dates. In the true story, Cumae, the first Greek colony in Italy, was built about 750 B.C., when Rome was already a country town with high hopes for its future. But the Greek pioneer towns grew quickly. They became large cities—cities with handsome houses, busy markets, schools, and tall white temples as splendid as any in Greece. Syracuse, on Sicily, became the largest city in the Greek world. Sybaris became the most luxurious, and so famous that for thousands of years anyone who loved pleasure and comfort was called a Sybarite. By 500 B.C., southern Italy and Sicily were so filled with Greeks that the area was called *Magna Graecia,* "greater Greece."

For the Etruscans and Italians who came trading, a visit to the Greek cities was an education. They learned about mathematics and science and an alphabet for writing down words. They saw money, instead of grain or cattle, used for trading. They took home delicately painted Greek pottery and tried to copy it in their own workshops. They began to add Greek columns and carvings to their Etruscan buildings. And the gods they knew by Etruscan names came to seem very like the old Greek gods. Jupiter, the king of the gods, was like Zeus. Juno was like Zeus' wife, Hera. Venus, the goddess of love, was as powerful and as fickle as Aphrodite.

But one god was changed. Ares, the god of war, was not a great god in Greece. In the city that became Rome, he was called Mars, and he was nearly as important as Jupiter. The people of that city had already sought Mars' aid when they helped the Greeks to defeat the Etruscans. Later, when they began to look with envy at the rich colonies in the south, they turned to Mars again. The Greeks' time in Italy was growing short.

LEGENDS SAY THAT A WOLF MOTHERED ROMULUS AND REMUS, ROME'S FOUNDERS.

The City of Romulus

900 B.C.-256 B.C.

IN THE time when savage warriors roamed the plains and mountains of Italy, there stood on six low hills, just south of the river Tiber, six clusters of round huts made of twigs and leaves stuck together with mud. Each was a little town, the home of barbarian tribesmen. They herded cattle on the plain below, chased the wild pigs in the woods, and tried to make things grow in their marshy fields. Although the towns were always fighting or stealing cattle and sheep from each other, they shared a market place in a clearing beside the river. They also shared a crude fortress of heaped-up earth and rocks on a seventh hill. The huts on the hills, the market place, the fortress—this, about 900 B.C., a hundred years or so before the Etruscans came to Italy, was Rome.

Then a powerful chief came to the place of the seven hills. When he had built a great hut of his own, on the widest of them, he called together the chiefs of the six towns. He told them that he planned to build a city on their hills, and that their towns would all be parts of it. Whether the old chiefs agreed to the plan or not, it was done.

On the day in April which was the feast day of Pales, the guardian god of herds and flocks, the new chief performed the solemn ritual of the founding of his city. With a bronze plow, drawn by a cow and a bull yoked together, he dug one furrow—a sacred line that marked the city's boundaries, the place where its walls would be built. He traced the lines of two main streets—one running north-and-south, one east-and-west, and crossing in the market place beside the River

THE FURROW OF THE SACRED PLOW MARKED ROME'S BOUNDARY.

Tiber. Then, on the Capitol, the tallest of the seven hills, he dedicated new huts as homes for Jupiter and Juno and Minerva, the gods whose protection he begged for the new city.

ROMULUS AND REMUS

No one knows where the great chief came from, or when he plowed his sacred line around the city. The people of five of the old villages were Latins. They were members of the tribe which claimed all of the broad plain, Latium, south of the Tiber River. The sixth village belonged to men from another tribe, the Sabines. But the gods of the new city had Etruscan names, so perhaps the new chief was an Etruscan king.

The Romans told a story that answered all of the questions. It began in a little town called Alba Longa, a place where the Latins once had a temple to their old gods. There, the Romans said, twin boys were born—Romulus and Remus. They were not ordinary children. Their mother was a descendant of Aeneas and their father was the god Mars. For the king at Alba that made them dangerous. He was afraid that when these children of a god grew up, they would be strong enough to steal his throne just as he himself had stolen it from the children's grandfather. The king ordered his servants to kidnap the babies and to leave them on the bank of the Tiber to die. The servants did as he commanded, but Romulus and Remus did not die. They were discovered by a she-wolf, who carried them to a field and mothered them like her own cubs until a shepherd found them and took them home to his wife.

Grown to manhood, the twins were everything the king had feared they might be: as fierce as the wolf who had mothered them, as noble as their ancestor Aeneas, and almost as strong as their father, Mars. They killed the wicked king. Then they left Alba Longa and went back to the field where they had lived with the wolf, to build a city of their own. As they began to plan its walls, they argued. Each had his own design for the city, and each wanted his own way. They tried to settle things peacefully by asking the gods to send a sign that would show which of them was right. When Remus prayed for the gods to vote for him, six eagles suddenly appeared in the sky, circled above their heads, and flew away. But when Romulus prayed, twelve eagles appeared.

"You see the sign of the gods!" Romulus shouted. "If I am king, our city will stand for twelve hundred years. But if you are king, it will last only half as long."

Remus refused to accept the eagles as signs. Furious, he tried to murder his brother, but was killed himself. So it was Romulus alone who marked out the boundaries of Rome with the sacred bronze plow. He did it, according to the tale, on April 21, the feast day of the god Pales, in 753 B.C.

GROWTH OF THE CITY

That was the story. April 21 was always celebrated as the birthday of the city, and the wolf became its symbol, an animal sacred to Mars. For nearly eight hundred years a crude round hut, which people called the "House of Romulus," stood among the shining white buildings that were built on the Palatine Hill. All that anyone knew for certain was that once there were six villages, but by 600 B.C. there was a thriving city. It was ruled by kings, until the last of them,

ANCESTORS AND HOUSEHOLD GODS WERE HONORED IN ROMAN HOMES.

an Etruscan, was driven out by the Romans in 509 B.C.

What happened during the four hundred years between remained a mystery, but the changes brought by those years were plain enough. By 509 B.C., the soggy fields had been drained and planted with vegetables, fig trees, olives, and grapevines. There were more sheep and fatter cattle. A strong new fortress had been built, as well as a handsome temple on the hill called the Capitol.

All this looked like the work of Etruscans. But the city's people were not Etruscans, except, perhaps, for a few colonists who had stayed behind when the king was driven away. Most of the people were Latins from the old villages, and Sabines, and some were wanderers who had drifted into the city and stayed. But what they had been did not matter. Now they lived in Rome; now they were all Romans. They were different from any people the world had known before—proud, strong, courageous, and practical. These Romans were men who looked at life as a series of jobs to be done: a field to be planted, a house to be built, a family to be raised, a country to be conquered. The bigger jobs simply took more effort.

THE LIFE OF A ROMAN

One such Roman was Publius Tullius Servius. His story was in his name: Publius, his own name, the one his friends used; Tullius, the name of his clan, the tribe of his ancestors; and Servius, his family name, the name of his father and of his father's father. It was good to have such a name, for it proved that Publius came from an ancient, respected family. It reminded everyone he met of the famous deeds of his parents and grandparents. Rome was old-fashioned about such things, and people honored most the men whose ancestral histories were the longest. In politics, business, or society, nothing mattered more than a man's family.

Publius and his own family lived in a one-room house built of clay bricks. Though they were far from poor, the room served them as living room, bedroom, kitchen and dining room. Romans did not go in for luxuries. At mealtimes, the family gathered around the table set next to the hearth, which was in the center of the floor. Their dinner was simple—wheat or oatmeal cakes, vegetables, a glass of wine, and fruit. Meat was for special occasions only. But what they had, they shared with the gods. Little clay statues of the *Penates*, the friendly spirits who looked after the food cupboard, were placed on the table so that they could feel that they were a part of the family. Bits of food and some wine were dropped into the fire as offerings to the goddess Vesta, who protected the hearth and all the household.

Vesta and Janus, the gatekeeper who guarded the door, were the most important of the family gods, but there were dozens of others. They were not the adventurous gods the Greeks had known, but practical minded, like the Romans who worshiped them. Each had his job to do and his price for getting it done—a sacrificed animal, or an offering of honey, cheese, or milk. When Publius went out to his fields in the spring, he prayed to Terminus, the god who looked after the boundaries of the farm, and then to Seia, who watched the corn seed in the ground. As summer began and the corn grew tall, Publius prayed to Flora, because it was her job to take care of the flowering corn. When the ears of corn were ripe, he turned to Runcina, who watched over the harvesting, and finally to Tutilina, who kept it safe in the barn.

There were many more of these useful gods, and with each of them Publius made a bargain. He promised to make a certain offering in return for a job well done, but he did not give it until after that job had been performed. If something went wrong, he did not pay the god at all. That was common sense, Roman sense.

Publius and his fellow Romans treated the gods of the city, great and small, in nearly the same way. They looked to Janus to guard its gate and had built him a temple, like a huge gateway in the Forum, the old market place. Its great doors, the "Gates of War," were left open in times of war; when there was peace, they were closed. Nearby was the round temple of Vesta, with the sacred hearth of the city. A group of priestesses, the Vestal Virgins, tended the fire that was never allowed to go out.

On the Capitol Hill stood the great temple of the three gods who had been Rome's protectors since the day of its founding—Jupiter, the sky king; Minerva, the goddess of wisdom and art; and Juno, whose special care was for women and babies. Vulcanus, the rumbling god of earthquakes and volcanoes, had his own temple. Publius was not slow to make his offerings there. Like every Roman, he paid what was due and added strong prayers, for Vulcanus was already too busy in Italy. A field outside the city wall, the Campus Martius, where the soldiers marched and practiced battle maneuvers, was dedicated to the special Roman god, Mars. He was worshiped as the god of planting as well as the god of war. That, too, was good sense—in the ancient world both activities usually got started in his month, March.

THE DUTIES OF A FATHER

Among all these gods of Publius' city, there was not one whose job it was to tell the Romans how to behave. That was the duty of their fathers. As the father of a Roman family—the *pater familias*— Publius Tullius Servius was a king in his home. He had the power of life and death over his wife, his children, and his slaves. Their behavior was his responsibility. He owed it to his ancestors and to Rome to teach them to act honestly, nobly and bravely, and to punish them if they did not. The Romans told many stories

THE VESTAL VIRGINS TENDED THE SACRED HEARTH OF THE CITY.

YOUNG ROMANS TRAINED THEIR BODIES THROUGH SPORTS.

about fathers who had killed their own sons for cowardice or disobedience.

Like most of the men he knew, Publius tried to be as fair as he was strict. When there were serious problems, he discussed them with his family before he decided what to do. The law said that his wife was his property, like his house, his cattle, or his slaves, but he treated her as his partner. His house was hers to manage, and their children hers to love. Like all Romans, they wore only clothes made in their own household, and Publius' wife saw to the making of them. She was free to go about the city as she liked, and Publius never asked her, as Greek husbands did, to stay out of sight when his friends came to dinner. His feelings for his wife were like those of another, who had carved these words on his wife's gravestone:

Stranger, what I have to say is short, so stay and read. Here is the unbeautiful grave of a beautiful woman. Her parents named her Claudia. She loved her husband with her whole heart. She bore him two sons: one she left alive on the earth, the other she buried in the earth. Her speech was gay, but her bearing seemly. She kept the home. She made the wool. I have spoken. Now go.

Publius' most important job was the education of his sons. They had no school, and no tutor but their father. He taught them the sports that would make them strong—running, swimming, boxing, and wrestling. As soon as they could wield sticks and little wooden daggers, he began to teach them war games, too, for every Roman citizen had to serve in the army. He told them

WAR GAMES HELPED PREPARE THEM FOR SERVICE IN THE ARMY.

about their ancestors, and the wax masks of their faces which hung on the walls of the house to show that they were still honored members of the family. On holidays, the masks were taken down and carried to the celebrations. They were taken to every important family ceremony, for the Romans had the old Etruscan fear of the spirits of the dead and they were careful not to insult an ancestor whose ghost might be hovering about.

A PRACTICAL EDUCATION

As Publius' sons grew older, he took them with him when he went to his fields or about the city on business. In that way, they could learn by watching him. All of their training was practical, and all of it was serious. Discipline was what made the difference between a Roman and any other man. "Obey the command," Publius would say, "act as a Roman, and die to save Rome, our family, or your own honor." Nothing was studied because it was fun or just interesting. Philosophy and poetry were for the Greeks. The only stories Publius told his children were about the Roman gods and heroes.

He told them about Romulus and the sacred plow and the family of the Roman state. When Romulus built his city, Publius said, he chose the finest men to be his soldiers, the legions who marched behind the silver eagles mounted on standards. One hundred of these men, the best and the richest, he made his counselors. He called them senators and told them to look after the poorer and weaker men of his city. And to these lesser men, Romulus also gave a duty: to

AN OFFICIAL ON HIS WAY TO THE SENATE WITH HIS GUARDS, CALLED *LICTORS*

love and honor his senators as fathers, the patrons of Rome.

When the Romans chased the Etruscan king from their city, the senators took charge of the government. They served so wisely that visitors from other countries called them "the council of kings." Each year they elected two men as consuls, presidents of Rome, who managed the city and commanded the armies. As the city grew, other officers were elected. Four officials called quaestors, for example, assisted the consuls. Censors kept track of the people by taking a "census" and "censored" their conduct by punishing them when they misbehaved or broke the laws.

Over the years, the senators and officials became the aristocrats of Rome. They owned much of its land, and made the laws, and many of them began to look with contempt at the noisy "children" they were supposed to look after. The other citizens, in turn, began to complain about "city fathers" who told them what to do but never consulted them. Then the people went on strike. One morning they simply walked out of the city. They refused to come back unless the senate agreed to treat them like men and with proper respect.

The strike not only left Rome empty, but without an army. The senators rushed to make an offer that would bring the citizens back. They would let an assembly of the people vote about some of the city's business, they said. The assembly would elect tribunes, who would have the power to veto anything done by any other official, even the consuls. A committee was appointed to write down the laws of Rome and to set them out on bronze tablets in the Forum, where everyone could see them and know his rights as a citizen.

THE RISE OF THE REPUBLIC

The people accepted the senators' offers and returned to the city. They called two or three more strikes before things were settled to their satisfaction, but out of the arguments and the political deals grew the Roman Republic, the new family of citizens. Its rules were the Laws of the Twelve Tablets, posted in the Forum. Its strength was in the old Roman virtues which every father was expected to teach his sons: honor, good sense, and the courage to get on with a job no matter how difficult or dangerous it was. The job of running the city was still divided between the city fathers in the senate and the commoners in the assembly, but they tried to work together. So long as they did, the Republic and Rome were strong.

These were the lessons Publius taught his sons, for he had served as a consul and was now a senator. He hoped that his sons, too, would some day serve as city officers. Rome needed good leaders; it was growing more powerful every day and many other cities looked to it for leadership. All of the Latin tribes of Latium had allied themselves to Rome. In 493 B.C. they signed a contract of friendship:

> *Let there be peace between the Romans and all the Latin cities so long as heaven and earth are still in the same place. Let them never make war on each other, but help each other with all their force when attacked, and let each have an equal share of all the spoil and booty won in wars they fight together.*

Now other towns in Italy were making contracts with Rome, for they shared many dangers. In his youth, Publius had lived through the awful years when fierce, barbaric Gauls had swept down from the Po Valley in the north. In 390 B.C., they had taken Etruria and invaded Rome itself. All of the city had been captured except the citadel on the Palatine Hill. That ancient fortress had never fallen, and finally the Gauls had given up trying to take it. But they did not leave Rome until the citizens had suffered the shame of buying back their own city with a ransom of gold.

Publius and his friends in the Senate swore that such a thing would never happen again. They had a great new wall set up around Rome and added thousands of men to the army. Publius said that if his sons served their city and its legions as true Romans should, then his sons' sons would see Rome conquer the whole of Italy.

ROME CONQUERS NEW LANDS

As it turned out, Publius proved to be right. The Gauls, who had taken Rome's gold and gone away, were the last barbarians to invade the city for eight hundred years. About 350 B.C., the Samnites, the savage tribesmen who held the mountains that ran south along the peninsula, attacked their kinsmen in the lowlands and threatened Rome. The legions marched out of the city, chased the invaders back to the hills, and won for Rome the great plain of Campania with its wealthy city, Capua. Then the Latins, afraid of Rome's new strength, tried to break the old contract of friendship. When they went to war about it, Roman armies swept down on their little towns,

IN THE SENATE, THE PATRICIANS DEBATED AND MADE LAWS FOR THE CITY.

THE APPIAN WAY, WITH A CROSS-SECTION OF THE ROAD AT LEFT

forcing them to agree to fight beside the Romans instead of against them.

That was in 353 B.C. In the same year, Philip of Macedon, the father of Alexander the Great, conquered the city-states of mainland Greece. While he and his son dreamed of building an empire in the East, the practical Romans were laying the foundations for an empire that would spread in every direction.

It began with cities and with roads. The Latin towns had a special place in the Roman plan. Their people were Rome's closest allies and had "Latin Rights" which gave them some of the privileges of Roman citizens. There were colonies too, because wherever the legions went, Roman settlers followed. Dozens of new towns sprang up at river crossings and ports, and on the hills that commanded the richest fields in Italy. In times of peace, they added to Rome's wealth; in times of war, they were headquarters for the armies. Their people were full citizens of the Republic. There was another sort of arrangement for the old Italian towns which agreed—or were forced—to make contracts with Rome. The Italians fought for Rome, but kept their own governments and officials. They could become citizens of Rome only by moving to the city itself.

For over a century, the Gates of War stood open in the Forum, and the list of towns tied to Rome grew longer and longer. With so many places to look after, the Romans needed a way to move their troops quickly. In 312 B.C., the senator Appius Claudius Caecus began to build a highway between Rome and Capua. It was called the Appian Way, and was the first of the great Roman roads. It was straight, level, weatherproof, and built to last almost forever. On a foundation of stones, the Roman engineers poured crushed rocks, bound them together with a thick layer of cement, then covered it all with smooth paving stones so carefully fitted together that water could not seep between them. The Appian Way crossed the rivers on great stone bridges. A viaduct carried it over the Pontine Marshes. No one in the world had built such roads before, and not until the coming of the railways did anyone find a better method of moving men and goods by land. When the Appian Way was finished, the Romans planned a network of highways—to Brundisium and the seaports in the south, to the ancient cities in Etruria, and north as far as Arminium on the coast of the Adriatic.

Meanwhile, as the roads and armies moved down the peninsula, the Greeks in the southern

cities became frightened. They wanted no "contracts" with anyone, especially Rome, but they knew the strength of the legions. In 280 B.C., the Greek cities hired an army of 20,000 men from the Peloponnesus to defend them and asked Pyrrhus, the most famous Greek general of the time, to take command.

THE DEFEAT OF PYRRHUS

Pyrrhus was another man who dreamed of winning an empire. His followers called him the "Eagle." When he sailed to southern Italy to fight the Romans, he was certain he was taking the first step toward setting up a western empire. The twenty elephants he brought with him were meant to remind his enemies that he was a sharp, up-to-date commander from the East, like Alexander. After all, he said, the Romans were only barbarians.

The Eagle met the Roman legions on the battlefield, defeated them, and offered them peace. To his great surprise, Rome refused and raised another army. Pyrrhus defeated it, too, but his own casualties were high. "Another such victory," he said, "and we are lost." So he left Italy to try his luck against Rome's allies, the Carthaginians, in Sicily.

In 275 B.C., he was back. Rome had raised a third army, and this time Pyrrhus' clever strategy could not overcome the dogged courage of the soldiers he had called barbarians. The Roman wolf broke the Eagle's wings, and Pyrrhus gave up the fight. As he limped away from the Italian plain where his dreams of empire had been ruined, he thought of the great new powers he had seen in the West. Rome was only one of them; perhaps it was the strongest. Pyrrhus sighed. "What a glorious battlefield I leave to Carthage and Rome," he said, and took his elephants home to the Peloponnesus.

One by one, the cities surrendered. By 256 B.C., Rome controlled them all. The new roads were extended to Cumae, Neapolis, Sybaris, and the rest, and Romans began to say, "All roads lead to Rome." This was certainly true of Italy, for the Romans had conquered the entire peninsula. But in Rome itself, the Gates of War were still not closed. Many kings and cities were jealous of Rome's power. None of them was more anxious to do something about it than Carthage. New wars were brewing, and Pyrrhus' prophecy about the battlefields of Italy would soon come true.

The City of Dido

264 B.C.-129 B.C.

In 264 B.C., the people of Rome met in a noisy session of their assembly. The question before them was: "Peace or War?" The Roman legions had proved their strength in winning all of Italy. Now the time had come to decide whether or not to risk the troops in wars away from the peninsula.

Meeting with the assembly was a representative from Messana, an independent town on Sicily, just across the narrow channel from the tip of Italy. Troops from Carthage had attacked the town and captured it. Now Messana begged for help from Rome. The Senate, knowing well the power of Carthage, wanted to say no. But in the assembly were many men who had fought in the legions, men who were proud and sure of their strength. When the arguments dragged on, they clamored for a vote, and the assembly voted for war. Dido's curse—the burning hatred between her city of Carthage and Rome, the city of Aeneas—had come true at last. Even if the legend of Dido was only a story, the war itself was curse enough. From one Sicilian town it spread to half of the Mediterranean, a full-scale war between the greatest powers of the West. Once begun, it went on for 119 years, and ended only when one of the two powers was utterly destroyed.

Carthage was perhaps the richest city in the world, the international headquarters of merchant-princes who could afford to buy anything—luxu-

THE PORT OF CARTHAGE, BUSY WITH MERCHANT VESSELS, WAS GUARDED BY A STRONG FLEET OF BATTLESHIPS. AT RIGHT, A CARTHAGINIAN MASK OF THE 2ND CENTURY B.C.

ries, men, ships, or cities. It was three times the size of Rome. It had rows of magnificent buildings, and two fine harbors, one for merchant vessels and one for ships of war. The city was just as famous, however, for its dishonesty and cruelty. The god of Carthage was Baal, a greedy, cruel god of gold and fire. His great bronze statue in the center of the city held out its hands to receive human sacrifices and feed them into the flames on its sacred hearth.

A NAVY FOR ROME

But Baal had brought luck to his people. Their city stood beside the narrow stretch of ocean that was squeezed between Sicily and the African coast. Taking control of the channel, the Carthaginians had cut the Mediterranean in two, and made the western half their own. Their colonies dotted the shores of Spain, North Africa, and Gaul. The island of Corsica was theirs, and Sardinia and much of Sicily. To guard these valuable possessions, they had the strongest fleet of battleships in the world.

The Romans who voted to go to war with this great sea power had no navy at all. Being Romans, however, they saw they had another job to do—and did it. In two months' time, with one captured battleship to study and some Greek sailors to advise them, they built a fleet of more than one hundred five-decked ships of war. While the ships were being built, Italian farmers learned seamanship by sitting on benches on the sand and practicing rowing.

When the ships were ready and the rowers at last put their oars into water, the new navy sailed south. In the first battle, the untried Roman seamen defeated a Carthaginian fleet. Some of the credit for the victory went to an improvement the

Romans had added to their ships: a drawbridge, fastened near the prow of each vessel, with a hook at its free end. When a Roman ship pulled close to an enemy warship, the bridge was dropped, its hook slammed into the enemy's deck, and Roman marines dashed across to attack.

THE WAR WITH CARTHAGE

The war, which had begun on land, became a series of the greatest naval battles ever fought in the ancient world. When a storm wrecked their entire navy, the Romans built another. But when these ships were sunk by a fleet from Carthage, there was no money in the state treasury to pay for building more. A Roman army was left stranded in Africa and miserably beaten. Carthaginian raiders sailed boldly along the Italian coast, attacking the towns and harbors.

Then the Roman citizens dug into their own pockets and their wives gave up their jewelry. Another army was raised, and 200 more ships were somehow built and paid for. When the new fleet put to sea, it hunted down the ships from Carthage, sank many of them, and chased the others back to Africa. Carthage was forced to beg for peace. It offered to give up its claims to the cities in Sicily, and the Romans agreed. They were tired and desperately needed time to build up their strength. Twenty-three years of war had cost them 500 ships and the lives of 200,000 men.

"Rome loses battles, but never a war," the Romans liked to say—and they often proved it. Defeated, the Roman wolf licked its wounds, got to its feet, and attacked again. When one army was destroyed, two more seemed to spring from the earth to take its place. Rome's soldiers came from the farms and hills of Italy in almost endless numbers. When the Romans had first captured the towns on the peninsula, they had had the good sense to make the people their allies rather than their slaves. They had given some, like the Latins, special rights in the Republic. Now Rome could count on these cities to add cavalry and archers to its own enormous armies.

Rome could also count on the courage of its soldiers. They were disciplined as well. The consuls elected to command the armies were the only law once the troops left Rome, and execution the only punishment for neglect of duty, disobedience, or cowardice. Few Roman soldiers were tempted to run to escape death on the battlefield.

In battle, every man was well protected by the tight, well-ordered formations which Roman armies always used. Legions made up of 4,500 men or more were divided into 1,200 light infantrymen, 3,000 heavy infantrymen who carried both javelins and heavy short swords, and 300 horsemen. On the battlefield, the heavy infantry, the main fighting force, was drawn up in three lines: young soldiers in the first line, seasoned men in the second, and veterans of long experience in the third. In each line there were gaps between companies, covered by the line ahead or behind. If the fighting was hard, the tired young men of the first line pulled back through the gaps, and the next line went at the enemy. If still more force was needed, the third line moved up. Horsemen and light infantrymen were also drawn up in strict formation. A Roman legion was a huge war machine in which every soldier had his place. He did his job and kept to his formation. He went on fighting until he was killed, or the enemy surrendered, or his captain changed the orders.

When the war with Carthage broke out again, as it did when both sides had had time to recover their strength, Rome's power was in its well-disciplined troops. Year after year, hundreds of thousands of men came from the countryside to fill the legions. The Carthaginians had no such endless supply of soldiers. Against the legions, Carthage's strength was strategy, the skillful maneuvering of troops that makes it possible for a small army to defeat a big one. The new war became a contest between Roman power and the brilliant strategy of one Carthaginian commander, Hannibal.

Hannibal had known soldiering and war from his childhood. His father, the great general Hamilcar, had taken him along on the campaigns he led against the Spaniards. Rome and Carthage were officially at peace, but the Carthaginians still hated Rome. At nine, Hannibal swore that he would be Rome's enemy as long as he lived. At the age of twenty-six, he was given the Spanish command his father had held, and was determined to make good his oath.

The campaign Hannibal planned against Rome was so bold and daring that his officers gasped when they heard it. With Rome in control of the

NAVAL BATTLES PLAYED A MAJOR ROLE IN ROME'S WAR AGAINST CARTHAGE.

THE ROMAN LEGIONS OUTNUMBERED THE CARTHAGINIANS THIRTY TO ONE, BUT HANNIBAL, USING ELEPHANTS, DEFEATED THEM TIME AFTER TIME.

seas, Hannibal said he would attack by land, taking his army through the Pyrenees Mountains at the top of Spain, then west across Gaul, and over the Alps into northern Italy. By 218 B.C., all his preparations had been made, and he started out from Spain with an army of 40,000 Spaniards and Numidian horsemen.

When the news reached Rome, the city's generals and military advisers were not greatly worried. Hannibal's plan was impossible, they said. They decided, however, to take no chances. They sent an army to stop him when he reached Gaul. But Hannibal bypassed the Roman army; he was saving his men for the fight in Italy. The Roman commanders in Gaul decided to go on to Spain and attack the troops Hannibal had left behind. The mountains, they said, were defense enough for Italy.

HANNIBAL CROSSES THE ALPS

Hannibal came to the Alps in early autumn and began the climb up the steep, treacherous trails just as the first snows were falling. The long line of his army wound around the white mountains. It went along the edges of ravines where a man's misstep meant death, and through narrow passes where the rocks had to be chipped away to allow the war elephants to get through. Hannibal seemed to be everywhere along the line, urging on his hungry and half-frozen soldiers. He supervised the hauling of animals and supplies up the mountains, and spoke the solemn words of farewell at the brief funerals of the men who died along the trail.

Late in September, he brought his army into the Po Valley at the northern end of Italy. He had done the impossible; he had defeated the Alps. It was a victory that matched the triumphs of Alexander. But he had not yet fought the war he had come to fight, and only 26,000 of his 40,000 troops had come through the mountains alive. Against these, Rome could call up 770,000 citizen-soldiers and allies.

Two great armies marched north from Rome, planning to crush Hannibal's forces before they could leave the Po Valley. Instead, the Romans were taught a bitter lesson in battle tactics. With his tired, outnumbered men, Hannibal outflanked the confident legions and chopped them down. The message that the Romans sent back to the Senate was short: "We have fought a great battle and we have been defeated."

It seemed that Hannibal had only to march to Rome to conquer it. But he did not go to the city. He had no heavy war machines—the catapults and battering rams needed to break down the defenses of a great city—and Rome's defenses were strong. That became the story of the war, year after year. Hannibal's strategy brought him victories whenever he met a Roman army on the field, but he could not touch the city. And Rome, though safe from capture, was unable to field an army—or a commander—that could win a battle against Hannibal.

Meanwhile, Hannibal could go where he liked on the peninsula. He spent the winter in the north, giving his men a rest. In the spring, he headed south and, on the way, destroyed two more armies from Rome. Never before had the Roman Republic suffered such costly defeats or faced such danger. The senate and the assembly agreed to appoint a dictator, Fabius Maximus, to take charge of the city's defenses. Fabius knew Rome's strength and weaknesses well, and he tried to explain them to the citizens. It was wrong, he said, to send more men to be killed by Hannibal. Rome could win the war only by waiting; sooner or later, Hannibal would run out of soldiers and supplies. But the Romans were impatient and refused to take his sensible advice. They called him *Cunctator,* "the slow-poke."

New commanders were elected, men who were anything but slow to act. They marched an army of 54,000 soldiers south to a place called Cannae—straight into a trap. When the two enemies came onto the field, the armies of both were in strange new formations. The companies of Roman soldiers were not arranged in the usual checkerboard pattern. Instead, they were massed together in huge, tight blocks. Their commanders, sure of their strength in numbers, meant to drive these blocks of men straight into Hannibal's front line, push it back, and smash it.

THE BATTLE OF CANNAE

But Hannibal, too, had a plan. He knew that he was weak in numbers. He also knew that his cavalry was better than that of the Romans, and he intended to take advantage of both his weakness and his strength. He strung out his Spanish and Gallic infantry along the center of his line, knowing that they would be pushed back. But he placed his Libyan cavalry on either side of them and his crack Carthaginian horsemen at the ends.

The Romans attacked. The mass of legionaries rumbled across the field, crashed into the enemy line, and pushed. In the center, the Gauls and Spaniards fell back, but the Libyan cavalrymen held their ground. Under the pressure of the attack, the line slowly bent until it was shaped like a crescent—with the Romans inside the curve. Then the Libyans began to move toward the center, drawing the crescent more tightly around the legionaries.

The wind whipping across the field blew dust into the Romans' faces and the sun shone into their eyes. Again Hannibal had planned wisely. He had placed his men on the field to take advantage of the prevailing wind and the position of the sun. Furthermore, the legionaries were packed together so closely that they could hardly swing their swords. Hannibal had not foreseen this; it was a gift to him from the Roman commanders who had ordered the new formation.

While the Roman infantrymen were pushing forward, the Carthaginian horsemen scattered the Roman cavalry. Now the Carthaginian cavalry turned back, attacking the Roman footsoldiers and turning the crescent into a deadly circle. The ranks of legionaries broke in confusion, but there was no way for them to escape. Hannibal's troops closed in and cut them down.

For Hannibal, it was a splendid victory, proof again of his skill in the arts of war. But for Rome it was a disaster, the greatest in the city's history. Twenty-five thousand Romans were killed at Cannae and 15,000 were taken prisoner. And the battle had other results. As the news spread across Italy, many of the towns that had been Rome's allies decided to make peace with Hannibal. Wealthy Syracuse switched to the Carthaginian side, and then Capua opened its gates to Hannibal without a fight.

In the years that followed, the darkest of the war, the Romans at last decided to take Fabius' advice. When they had raised twenty-five new legions, they kept them safely away from Hannibal. They used them to attack the towns which he had captured or persuaded to desert the cause of Rome. A huge force was sent to besiege Syracuse. At Capua, a double circle of Roman armies sat outside the walls, waiting for the city to starve or surrender. The tide of war was beginning to turn.

Hannibal brought his soldiers to the gates of Rome and camped in the plain of Latium, hoping to frighten the citizens into calling home their troops. But they refused to be frightened. Inside the stout walls of the city, the people held an auction to sell the land on which he had built his camp. A Roman paid a good price for it, certain that he would have the use of it before long. When Hannibal turned his back on Rome and once more marched south, not one legionary had been called back from Syracuse or Capua. In 211 B.C., those two cities surrendered to Rome. Hannibal sent for reinforcements from Spain. They made their way through the Alps, but were met and destroyed by four Roman legions—the first defeat of Carthaginian troops in Italy.

SCIPIO TAKES COMMAND

Meanwhile, a young Roman officer named Scipio had begged to be given the command of the legions in Spain. Scipio was only twenty-five and he had never had full command of an army. But, like Hannibal, he had grown up in a world of soldiers. And, again like Hannibal, he came from a family of generals who had made their names fighting in Spain. His father and his uncle had been killed there. Now Scipio asked to be allowed to avenge their deaths. The citizens were impressed with his show of courage, and they gave him the command, hoping that he would know what to do. In three years, Scipio learned his way about Spain and won many of the Spaniards to the Roman side. He turned his half-trained soldiers into efficient fighting men, and pushed the Carthaginians into the sea. When he hurried home, eager to do more, the Romans knew that they finally had a commander to match their troops.

Scipio asked for an army to invade Africa and attack Carthage itself. The expedition set out in 204 B.C., and again the young commander led his army to victory. Twice he defeated the strongest forces which the Carthaginian merchants could hire to defend their city. Carthage, fighting for its life, now ordered Hannibal back to Africa. In 203 B.C., after fifteen years of campaigning in Italy, he sailed home. He had conquered the Alps, but not Rome.

In Africa, on a field near the town of Zama, he once more faced the Romans. But at Zama the legions were led by a general as young and as brilliant as Hannibal himself had been when he first invaded Italy. With Scipio, Rome had both numbers and strategy on its side; the contest between the two cities was no longer equal. At the

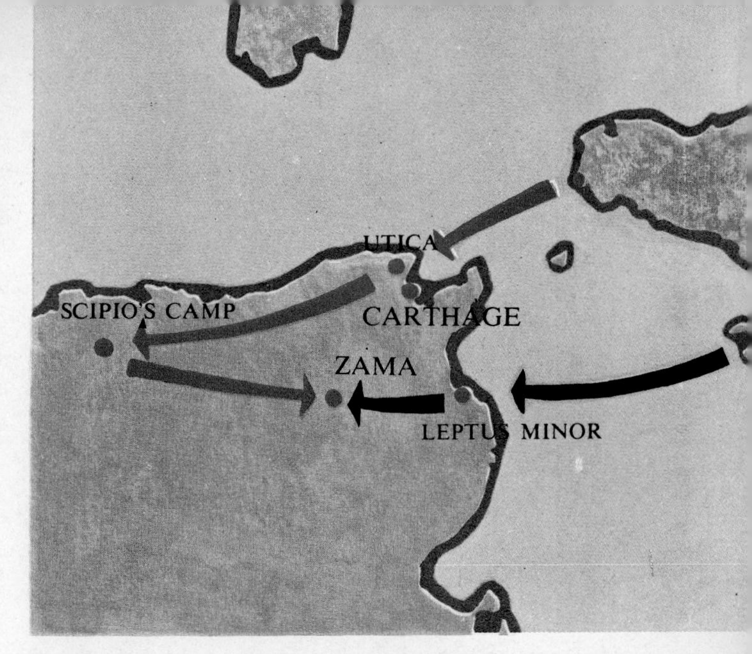

RETURNING FROM ITALY, HANNIBAL FOUGHT SCIPIO'S TROOPS AT ZAMA.

start of the battle, Scipio lined up his infantry and cavalry in almost the same formation which Hannibal had used at Cannae. Hannibal was prepared for that, but he simply could not match the strength. And, wherever he sent his soldiers during the long, terrible day of fighting, Scipio had shifted his men there first. Late in the afternoon, when the Carthaginian cavalry fled from the field, Hannibal called a halt to the slaughter and admitted he was beaten.

Carthage surrendered. Scipio sailed home to be honored in Rome with the new name Scipio Africanus, Scipio of Africa. Hannibal, too, went home—to share his city's defeat. But the Romans could not be comfortable while Hannibal was still free. They ordered the leaders of Carthage to hand him over to them. He fled to Syria, remaining there until that country, too, became dominated by Rome. Then, unwilling to be the prisoner of his sworn enemies, he killed himself. In the same year, 195 B.C., Scipio Africanus died.

But the Romans still feared the power of Carthage, which might some day attack them again. In the Senate, an old statesman, Cato, always finished his speeches with the words, "Carthage must be destroyed!" Many Romans agreed with him, and when they found an excuse to attack their old enemy, they voted for war again.

Roman soldiers camped outside Carthage for nearly three years before they managed to break through the thick walls and take the city. The people begged for mercy, but the Romans had

THE ROMAN TROOPS TOTALLY DESTROYED CARTHAGE. AT RIGHT: SCIPIO

been dreaming of revenge for too long. The 50,000 Carthaginians who lived through the street-fighting were rounded up and sold into slavery. The fortifications of their city and its rows of shining buildings were pulled to the ground. The great bronze statue of Baal was broken up, and the city set on fire. Roman priests solemnly prayed for the goddess Juno to leave the doomed city and to go to the temple which waited for her in Rome. Then a sacred plow was dragged through the ashes. Salt was sown in the scorched ground so that nothing would grow, and a curse was pronounced on any man who dared to build on it again. Thus the Romans marked the death of the richest city in the world.

THE POWER OF ROME

Africa became a Roman province, and in the same year—146 B.C.—Corinth in Greece was also demolished by the Romans. It was a reminder to the Greeks that they, too, were under the power of Rome. Macedonia, Alexander's old kingdom, had been made a Roman province two years earlier. Spain and some of Gaul already belonged to Rome. By 129 B.C., there was a Roman province in Asia, too, and even Egypt had decided that it was safer not to challenge a power that never lost a war.

In 264 B.C., when the Romans first voted to risk their troops in foreign lands, Rome was but one of five giants who jealously watched over the Mediterranean Sea. In the East, there were Egypt, Asia Minor, and Macedonia. In the West, besides Carthage, there was Rome, the youngest of the giants, untried and unknown. Kings, emperors, and cities of the East were tempted, like Carthage, to test the strength of the newcomer. Like Carthage, they met defeat. To the Romans, conquest was simply another job that had to be done.

By 129 B.C., only one power, Rome, held the Mediterranean Sea, and the Romans began to call it *Mare Nostrum,* "Our Sea."

The City Divided

130 B.C.-70 B.C.

MARCUS TULLIUS CICERO, a young statesman known for his dramatic speeches, stood before a panel of judges in a courtroom in Rome. He stared at them angrily. For fifty days he had travelled through Sicily, collecting facts about the crimes committed by Caius Verres, the man who was on trial. Now the judges had told him that there would not be time to listen to his evidence.

Cicero knew that the judges had been bribed. For it was no ordinary criminal that he meant to send to prison or to death. Caius Verres was an aristocrat and a senator, and had served for three years as the governor of the province of Sicily. Verres' lawyer was Hortensius, the leader of the aristocrats. Indeed, every rich or important man in Rome seemed to be supporting Verres. But Cicero was determined that this man should not escape judgment. He turned to Hortensius and offered to present his case in one day. "Would the court have time enough for that?" he asked sarcastically.

Hortensius was surprised, but he smiled and told Cicero to try it if he liked. The judges agreed.

For a moment there was silence in the courtroom, as Cicero turned to face the benches where the long lines of judges sat. Sternly he looked from man to man until he was certain all their eyes were on him. Then he began to speak. He listed Verres' crimes: When he was governor and the commander of Rome's army in Sicily, he had taken for himself the money raised to pay the troops. When he was governor and responsible for order and justice in the province, he had taken more money to allow pirates to rob the ports, to set criminals free, and to condemn innocent men. For gold, he had tortured and killed Roman

CICERO FOUGHT CORRUPTION WITH HIS DRAMATIC ORATORY.

AS THE POWER OF ROME GREW, ITS TOWNS AND CITIES ALSO GREW.

citizens who had the right to trial in Rome. When he was tax collector as well as governor, he had taxed the great Sicilian grain farmers until they starved. He had robbed the cities of their monuments, plundered their temples for gold, and stolen their Greek statues to decorate his own gardens in Italy. These things, Cicero said, were as well known in Rome as in Sicily. Caius Verres had boasted about them himself.

The court was silent. What Cicero said was true, and it was true of other governors as well. Verres was only among the worst of them.

Once more Cicero's voice rang out. Was it also true, he asked, that in Rome a rich man, whatever his guilt, could never be sent to prison for his crimes? Then Roman justice, not Verres, was on trial. Glaring at the judges now, Cicero asked them one last question. Did they dare to let Verres go free and so prove to the world that greed had destroyed the honor of Rome?

When Cicero sat down, the judges' faces were solemn. Hortensius' smile was gone and he made no answer to Cicero's speech. Cicero had won his case. When Verres heard how things had gone in court, he packed his gold and the best of his stolen statues, and fled from Italy.

The year of the trial was 70 B.C., sixty years after Rome had made itself the ruling power of the Mediterranean. The Romans were learning the lesson that Pericles' Athenians and the heirs of Alexander the Great had learned: winning an empire is difficult, but governing it wisely is more difficult still.

The conquered provinces looked to Rome for order and protection. Instead, they got governors who were out to make their fortunes and tax collectors who took money for themselves instead of for the government. Meanwhile, barbarians crashed across the frontiers. And closer to home, the Italian cities, Rome's first allies, grew more and more angry at giving their sons to be soldiers but never being allowed to vote. There were

RICH FAMILIES BUILT LARGE AND LUXURIOUS HOMES FOR THEMSELVES.

important jobs to be done, but the Republic—Rome's government of senators and commoners—was not doing them.

RICHES AND SLAVES

In the years when Rome was growing up, the Republic had weathered the storms of invasions and disasters. Time and again it produced men who saved the city and turned defeat into victory. But now, in the new, bigger world which Rome had conquered, the old system did not seem to work.

The city itself had changed. The simple houses of the old days were gone. The rich families of Rome now lived in big homes with many rooms and colonnaded courts, like the ones in Greece. Businessmen and politicians who had made fortunes in the provinces built palaces for themselves when they came home to Rome. They filled them with elegant imported furniture, decorated them with statues "borrowed" from temples in Greece, and bought dozens of slaves to do the household work.

The Romans had owned slaves almost from the first. Every farmer or craftsman had one or two to help out with his work. But the wars in Italy and the Mediterranean flooded the slave markets with captives: soldiers taken in battle, and men, women, and children from conquered cities. The war with Carthage brought more than 200,000 prisoners to Italy. The campaigns in the East brought almost half a million more. And in the rare times of peace, the supply of slaves was kept up by pirates, who raided little coastal towns and kidnaped their people. Capua, where half the shopkeepers in Rome bought their pottery and iron, became a great center for slave trading. Prices were low, and well-to-do Romans and farmers from all over the peninsula rushed to buy. A man whose father had been quite comfortable with two or three slaves to serve him now felt that he could not run his home without twenty or thirty. If he had an estate in the country as well as a house in town, he needed as many as three hundred.

When a man was sold as a slave, the kind of life he could expect depended on his skills and the temper of his master. The master was a matter of luck; one owner might whip his slaves and work them to death, while another would treat them with some kindness. But skills were a matter of education, and they made a great difference. The unskilled men and women who worked on farms or spent their days in the dark tunnels of the mines knew nothing but suffering. They slept in filthy huts, had only enough food to keep them working, and were often kept in chains. When they grew old or fell sick, no one did much about it. It was cheaper to let them die and buy young, healthy replacements.

But for a town slave, one who had talents or education, things could be very different. If he could cook well or curl his mistress' hair, talk philosophy or teach his master's children to read, he was a valuable possession and worth taking care of. Wealthy Romans were proud of showing off the skills of their best slaves—the scribes who copied their letters in an elegant hand, the singers who entertained their guests after dinner. A household of fine slaves gave a man standing. He saw to it that they were well fed and properly dressed so that no one would say that he was too poor to look after them.

A slave with a good head for business could earn more than food and clothes. His master might put him in charge of a little shop in the market. A portion of the profit was his to keep, and when he had saved enough money he could buy his freedom. Other slaves were given their freedom on the death of masters whom they had served well.

Most of these new "freedmen" stayed in Rome. They went into business for themselves as shopkeepers, craftsmen, or clerks. Some set up as doctors or teachers, and a few became millionaires. They added to the crowds in the booming foreign districts of the city, which now had nearly three-quarters of a million people.

Riches, slaves, and foreigners—they were changing Rome, and every change meant new trouble for the old Republic. The Romans themselves were changing most of all. Men from the oldest, most respectable families had taken to wearing soft, rich clothes instead of homemade togas. They stuffed themselves at banquets and clattered about the city in smart, new carriages. In summer, when Rome turned hot and dusty, they hurried off to Neapolis where their yachts were moored. They spent fortunes on jewelry for their wives, and bought Greek slaves to teach their children.

GREEK INFLUENCE GROWS

Rome was becoming very Greek. It showed in the statues and new houses. It showed, too, in the speeches in the senate and the law courts, for the plain-speaking Romans had become fascinated by the way the Greeks could talk. In war, a Roman knew what he was doing, but in battles of words, a clever Greek could turn his arguments inside out, making him look like a fool. The Romans soon saw how useful this could be in politics and business, and they wanted to learn how to do it themselves. When a *pater familias* planned the education of his sons, he usually saw to it that they learned Greek literature and rhetoric, the art of fine speech. Then he shipped them off to college in Athens.

Schools run by free Greeks sprang up all over Rome to teach the people who did not have the money or time to go to Greece. The ability to speak the Greek language, as well as to argue in the Greek fashion, became the sign of a man of intelligence and importance. Old-fashioned Romans objected to this "Greekness," and the softness and luxury that came with foreign ways. Old Cato, who had called so long and so often for the destruction of Carthage, had seen a new danger. "The truth," he said to anyone who would listen, "is that our possessions have captured us, and not that we have captured them!"

The Senate passed laws to limit the amount of gold jewelry a woman could wear and the number of guests her husband could invite to a banquet. Greek philosophers were outlawed in the city. But the new ways had come to Rome to stay. Cato himself finally learned to speak Greek, the philosophers returned, and the laws on jewelry and guests were forgotten. The Romans who could afford it went on enjoying themselves.

Not everyone, however, could afford it. The streets of Rome were full of penniless men, homeless and angry. They were drifters, discharged soldiers, and peasants whose small farms

GREAT ESTATES WORKED BY SLAVES REPLACED THE SMALL FARMS.

had gone to ruin while they served in the army. The slaves they had helped to capture made it possible for one rich farmer to run a great plantation without hired hands. The *latifundia*, the new, big farms, were made up of many little farms and land rented from the government. There was no place on them for the peasants, the men who had once been the backbone of Rome and the strength of its legions. The peasants left the country and came into the city. They could find no work there, either. But they discovered that in a Republic ruled by votes there was still power in numbers. The poor of the city became an unruly mob, shouting for attention, living on hand-outs from the government or from rich politicians, selling their votes in the assembly to the men who gave them the most. Without jobs, they had nothing to do with their time except wander the streets and make trouble. So the politicians began to give them free shows as well as free food.

The people flocked to the stadiums and to the racecourse called the Circus, and they liked their shows big. Their favorite sports were the cruelest ones—huge mock battles in which the deaths were real, and combats of gladiators, men who were sent into the arenas to kill. The Etruscans had once staged such deadly contests to provide their demon-gods with a sacrifice. In Rome, the fights were held for fun.

SOME GLADIATORS WORE LEATHER ARMOR AND HELMETS MADE OF BRONZE.

The gladiators were picked slaves, the toughest fighters among the prisoners of war. Barbarians from Africa and the north were in particular demand. In a prisonlike school for gladiators, they were trained for the arena. They were all taught to use the *gladius,* a short, sharp-pointed sword that could break a man's arm with one sideways blow or run him through with a thrust. Then the school rented them out to sponsors—the politicians who gave the shows in Rome.

If a gladiator was lucky, he lived through his first fights in the arena. He began to learn to kill with style and to show off his strength to please the crowd. That was important. When the great men in the city got to know his name and placed bets on him, they saw to it that he was pampered by his owner. As he became more famous, his fans showered him with presents. Schoolgirls screamed and fainted when he walked into the arena. But nothing could change the fact that winning today meant only a chance to risk his life again tomorrow.

As time went on, the marks of his trade showed on his body—scars, an ear half gone, a broken nose. Sooner or later, a younger, tougher fighter would turn up in the arena. The old favorite would be struck down and the people who had been his fans would shout for the new hero to finish him off. Until that happened, he had to go on fighting, knowing that in all the crowd only one person really cared if he lived or died. That was the sponsor, who got a refund for the gladiators he returned to the school undamaged.

THE SENATE AND THE MOB

A more expensive and livelier game was the "wild-beast hunt." Lions and elephants and other animals from Africa were strange and exciting to Romans. They liked to see them let loose in an arena with a group of prisoners who had to kill them or be killed. The men who planned the shows were always on the lookout for new ways to thrill the crowds. Rival politicians dug into their treasuries to hire more gladiators or wilder animals, and still the mob was not satisfied.

The people of the mob ran the Republic with their votes. Hungry and selfish, the mob hated the rich men and the senators, but needed them to live.

LARGE CROWDS CHEERED ON THEIR FAVORITES AT THE CHARIOT RACES.

The senators, proud and old-fashioned, used their power selfishly. They loathed the mob, but needed its votes and feared its anger. A third group, the knights, had once been Rome's cavalry; now they were the city's businessmen. They were rich, and willing to buy the votes of the mob or the senators to gain power for themselves. The disputes between the Senate and the people's assembly often gave them the chance.

At elections, there was violence and bloodshed in the streets. Rival groups and candidates tried to settle political contests with clubs and daggers. Rome still had wise and honest men, but when they tried to speak out they were shouted down by the mob, and the laws they tried to pass were voted down by the Senate. Sometimes they were murdered.

In 133 B.C., Tiberius Gracchus, a veteran officer, proposed a law to give land to his homeless soldiers. With land they could earn a living instead of begging. Not even the most selfish senator could deny that Rome owed them that much, he said. In the Forum, Tiberius told a cheering crowd, "Wild beasts have their lairs, but the men who fight and die for Italy can call nothing their own except the air and the sunshine!" The people's assembly elected him tribune, and the Senate hired a gang to kill him.

CAIUS GRACCHUS

Nine years later, his brother Caius tried again. In the hope that he could frighten the Senate with a show of money and power, he made pacts with businessmen and Rome's Italian allies as well as with the mob. At first things went well for him. He suggested laws which he thought would benefit everyone, and not just the poor. His program for finding usable land and establishing new colonies for the homeless won him the votes of the people. The businessmen and the Italians were pleased when he spoke of projects for building roads and harbors that would make jobs for the unemployed. Everyone agreed with him that the state ought to sell grain at low prices to those who could not otherwise afford to buy it. The people cheered him in the streets, and the Senate, truly frightened at last, did not dare to vote against him. Then he began to talk about votes for the Italians. It was time to treat them like proper citizens, he said. Suddenly his business friends

were much less friendly, and the mob turned on him. Votes were the only valuable thing they had; they did not intend to share them.

Riots broke out all over Rome as the people surged through the streets, howling for vengeance on Caius Gracchus. The senators, no longer afraid, issued an order for his arrest, and the mob was delighted to do the job for them. They joined the gang of slaves and thugs which the Senate had sent to hunt him down. When they had him trapped, they stood by while he killed himself. Caius' death was final proof that the mob could not be trusted even to help itself. It would take swords, not votes, to change the laws of the Republic.

From now on, when the people and the aristocrats of the Senate turned on each other, they would set out to destroy each other completely. And for leaders, they looked to the men who commanded armies. It had always been the rule in Rome that the Senate chose the generals. But in 107 B.C., the people overruled the senators. They picked their own man, Caius Marius, to command the legions fighting against Jugurtha, a rebel king in Africa. Caius Marius was a rough, country man, but a good officer. The people chose him because he promised that he himself would kill or capture Jugurtha, and because they were sure that he would never side with the Senate.

THE SOLDIERS' CHOICE

Marius was the soldiers' choice, too. They called themselves "Marius' Mules," for they were a corps of road builders and trench diggers as well as infantrymen. They carried eighty pounds of equipment on their backs when they marched across Africa. But so long as Marius led them, they did not complain. He was an old campaigner who ate at their table, shared their hardships, and knew war as they knew it. When he took command of the African legions, he began to build a new kind of army. He did not rely on the drafted citizens who had always filled the ranks. Instead, he took volunteers from

VICTORIOUS GENERALS WERE GIVEN TRIUMPHAL PROCESSIONS THROUGH THE CITY.

the penniless men of Rome. To them, the army meant a job. They were loyal to the officer who looked after them, not to the government that often had not. If he brought them victory and kept their stomachs full, they were his for so long as they lived.

The Roman mob was not that loyal, but, for the time being, Marius was their hero. When he returned victorious from Africa, they awarded him a "Triumph," the honor that Rome gave to its greatest generals. It was a grand procession, led off by the officers of the city and the senators. They were followed by the wagonloads of booty, and Marius himself, riding in a four-horse chariot. He was dressed in a robe of purple, which only victorious generals were allowed to wear. In his hand, he carried the laurel branch that he would place on Jupiter's altar as a sign of his success in war. Behind him marched his soldiers, chanting a song of victory, while the people cheered and hung garlands of flowers about their necks. It was a day of glory for Marius, but his glory was not

AS A BOY, MARIUS FOUND AN EAGLE'S NEST, AN OMEN OF FUTURE GREATNESS.

complete. One of his officers, a man named Sulla, had to be given credit for capturing the African king. Marius had meant to do that himself. His pride was hurt—and he was a man of great pride.

MARIUS AND SULLA

The people did not seem to care who had captured the rebel. They re-elected Marius consul, and went on re-electing him for four years. That had never happened before; consuls were supposed to change each year. But the people needed him, because hordes of new barbarians, more fierce than any that had come before, were attacking northern Italy.

Marius himself was not at all surprised at his honors and elections. He had expected them. When he was a boy, scrambling over the hills outside his village, he had found an eagle's nest with seven fledglings in it. A soothsayer, the wise man of the village, told him that it was a sign from the gods. He would win greatness seven times. A Roman soldier could win no greater honor than the post of consul-commander. As Marius marched north to face the barbarians, he never doubted that he would come back to Rome victorious. He was just as sure that the Romans would go on electing him until he had been consul seven times.

But when he had defeated the invaders and returned to the city, everything seemed to go wrong. The people began to change their minds about him. He was too proud, they said, and he had been consul too many times.

Marius could not understand it. In the field, he knew exactly what to do and when to do it; in the city, his blunt manners only got him into trouble. He had never learned to make fine speeches. He did not know how to deal with politicians. Even so, he was determined to be elected consul again. To win votes, he tried to please everyone, even the senators. The result was that he pleased no one, and lost the election. Marius did not take defeat easily. His pride was hurt, and he began to talk about revenge. To make matters worse, Sulla, the officer who had stolen his glory by capturing the African king, had become the favorite of the senate.

Suddenly, the Romans needed both Marius and Sulla. The people of the Italian cities were tired of waiting for the right to vote. They tore up the old agreements and declared war on Rome. Marius and Sulla were put in command of armies, and for three years they marched up and down the peninsula, fighting the men who had been their allies.

In Asia, an ambitious king, Mithridates, saw that here was a chance to win himself a new Persian empire. While civil war kept the Roman legions in Italy, he sent his troops into Syria and Asia Minor. The governors were helpless to stop them. Mithridates also sent secret agents into the Eastern cities where many Romans had settled. Quietly the agents organized the townspeople. Then, on one day of terror, the Asians attacked the westerners who had come to live among them. They murdered every Roman and Italian they could find—more than 100,000 men, women, and children, as well as their slaves.

In Rome, the citizens gasped at the news of the killings. A few weeks later, they had trouble of a different kind. Without taxes from Asia, the Roman treasury was soon all but empty. Millionaires, who depended on the eastern trade, found themselves penniless. The fight about voting began to look rather ridiculous. If Rome lost its provinces, ran out of money, and collapsed, voting would not matter very much. The Romans decided to end the civil war and, thanks to Mithridates, the Italians were given the full rights of citizenship.

LUCKY SULLA

The next question the Romans had to decide was who should command the army that must be sent to Asia. The Senate chose Sulla, but Marius wanted the command for himself. He was almost seventy years old, worn out, and often unable to control his fits of anger, but his pride was as fierce as ever. He went to the people and asked them to vote for him, against Sulla and the senators they hated. The mob did as he asked, then marched on the Senate, swearing to kill Sulla.

Sulla was too quick for them. He fled the city, but soon came back with his army and took Rome by force. Now it was Marius' turn to flee, and he had no army waiting in the country. Some of his followers left Italy with him, but when his money and provisions were gone, they deserted him. Alone, far from Rome and forced to live in hiding, he nursed his anger until it was close to madness. He dreamed of revenge and the day when he would command a Roman army again. If his courage faltered, he reminded himself of the sign of the seven eagles. Six times he had been consul. He knew that there would have to be a seventh time, and he waited.

Sulla, the new commander of the legions, was everything that Marius had never been. He had needed no soothsayers to tell him he would be great. He was Sulla Felix, "Lucky Sulla," a name he had chosen for himself because he was certain from the start that he was Fortune's favorite soldier.

It was true that things usually went Sulla's way. Though he was born poor, and his first home in Rome was a cheap room in a tenement, he came from an old, noble family. As a youth, he was handsome, with bright blond hair. He knew Greek, had a quick wit, and a way with people. He soon won a place in the politics and society of the city. He had no patience with the mob, and was sure that only the Senate could rule Rome. Even so, his soldiers learned to like him. He was bold, fearless, and could stand great hardship. When there were no battles to be fought, he liked to drink his wine, tell stories, and chase girls like any soldier.

After his trouble with Marius, however, Rome saw little of Sulla's pleasant side. When his army had brought order to the city again, he had Marius' friends rounded up and killed. Then he had a law passed that required the people's assembly to ask his permission before it could vote on anything at all. With these things done, he set off for his eastern campaign, leaving the Senate in charge of Rome. The senators soon ran into trouble. Cinna, a politician who sided with the people, was elected consul. When he took office, he invited Marius to come back to Rome. The Senate, with its general and his army across the Mediterranean, could do nothing about it.

The Marius who returned to Rome was not the man who had won the friendship of his soldiers in Africa. He was old, though every day he went down to the Campus Martius and exercised with the young men, showing them that he was still strong, still an expert horseman. He was bitter, and his dreams of revenge had made him cruel. When he had raised armies to send against Sulla's forces in the provinces, he built a private army for himself in Rome. He ordered the killing of hundreds of men who were said to be supporters of Sulla or the Senate. Then he began to order executions for no reason at all. One morning, a man who spoke to Marius in the street received no nod from him in return. In a moment, Marius' soldiers had grabbed the man. After that, if anyone greeted Marius and was not greeted in return, that person was killed. Even his old friends took to dodging around corners when they saw him coming.

The people, however, did not desert him. In 86 B.C., he was elected consul again. But his pleasure in that success was ruined by reports that

came from the East. Sulla was winning victories. Reports from still other areas told of Sulla's men defeating the armies that Marius had sent to destroy them. Marius grew sour and silent. Night after night he could not sleep. Then he fell sick; the anger burning in his mind seemed also to burn away his strength. In January, 86 B.C., he died, on the seventeenth day of his seventh consulship.

Three years later, Sulla returned to Rome and a triumphal procession. Up to this time, the victor's chariot had always followed the city officials and the senators. Sulla rode at their head. This was a difference that everyone noticed, and it was an important one. The Senate had already named him dictator of Rome; no man stood over or before him.

The years had changed him. His hair was no longer golden, and his pale skin was marked with red splotches. One witty Greek said he looked like "a mulberry sprinkled with meal." In the evenings, he was still the jolly soldier who loved a good party. He never forgot his friends, whether they were senators or scoundrels who lounged around the Forum. But by day, he was the dictator of Rome, merciless and cruel. While he was unbelievably generous with his friends, he was brutal to everyone else. Now his turn for revenge had come, and he ordered the execution of thousands of Marius' followers. When they were dead, he found other men to kill—men who had had nothing to do with politics. Some were killed because Sulla's friends owed them money, others because his friends wanted their fine houses or lands.

Sulla discovered a new and easy way to raise money—call a rich man a criminal, execute him, and claim his property. Each day a list of "men proscribed as criminals" was posted in the Forum. These men could be legally killed by anyone—indeed, the government would be grateful to the killer. Once the wealthy "criminals" were dead, Sulla's friends took charge of their gold and possessions. It was such an efficient system that, years later, dictators in other countries would copy it.

A NEW CONSTITUTION

And yet Sulla was always talking about "the good of Rome." While his henchmen chased down new victims, he worked at his favorite project—saving the Republic. He wrote a new constitution, which he hoped would bring back the good old days of fatherly senators and common citizens who did as they were told. "The laws, not I, will once again rule the good family of our state," he said to the people who lived in

SULLA'S VICTIMS WERE STRUCK DOWN EVEN IN THE TEMPLE COURTS.

terror of his orders—and he believed it. It did not occur to him that he himself had shown how little the wishes of the Senate mattered to a man who controlled the army. Nor did anyone dare to tell him that his murders for money had made law and justice a terrible joke. Instead, the Senate thanked him for the fine new constitution, which gave it complete power over the commoners. The people said nothing, and waited for a general who would write the sort of constitution they wanted, using his sword to make it law. Sulla resigned as dictator, confident that he had patched up the old Republic and that it would run itself again. Of course, he had his soldiers stand by, just in case.

In 79 B.C., he died, greatly mourned by the Senate and the friends he had helped to make so rich. They gave him a splendid funeral. As his body was carried through the streets at the head of his last triumphal procession, everyone cheered—his friends because they honored him, the others because he was dead. On his gravestone were carved the words he had chosen himself:

LUCIUS CORNELIUS SULLA—NO FRIEND EVER DID HIM A KINDNESS AND NO ENEMY A WRONG, WITHOUT BEING REPAID IN FULL.

The City of Caesar

80 B.C.-44 B.C.

THE story of Rome in the years after Sulla's death was the story of a partnership of power. It was the tale of three men who bargained for the world—a rich man, a poor man, and a man who was not only a hero, but looked it.

The rich man was Crassus, who had become a millionaire by setting up the only fire department in Rome. The tall buildings and narrow, crowded streets of the city made a fire a constant danger. When one house burned to the ground, the buildings on either side were likely to fall over on top of it. The cry of "Fire!" roused fear in the hearts of men whose wealth was in the buildings they owned. It was the signal, too, for Crassus and his fire-fighting slaves to come on the run. While the slaves got their equipment ready and looked for water, Crassus found the landlord of the burning building and offered to buy it from him. The price he offered was not high, but it was more than the house would be worth after it had been destroyed by fire. If the landlord refused to sell, Crassus shrugged and let the fire burn. Usually, however, the landlord sold and the firemen went to work. When the fire was out, Crassus sent a crew of carpenters to repair the damage. He soon had a building as good as new and worth a great deal more than he had paid for it. If he had talked fast enough, he also owned the buildings next door, which did not even need repairing.

Despite such dealings, Crassus was a popular man in the city. He was a good host. In politics, he took the side of the people, and he greeted the poorest citizen like an old friend. He was actually eager to lend money even though he charged no interest. Of course, he expected to be paid back in time, and many men—especially politicians—found themselves in debt to him. Crassus was as pleasant to them as before, and simply suggested that, until they could afford to repay the loan, they might lend him their voices and votes at election time. For Crassus wanted to be something more than the richest man in Rome; he wanted to be the most powerful, as well. He dreamed of himself in glittering armor, fearlessly leading the legionaries to victory over a foreign king. Then, returning to Rome, he would put on the purple robe of a conqueror and ride in triumph through the streets. The citizens would proclaim him their hero, the consul-commander who would rule them for as long as he lived.

SPARTACUS LEADS A REVOLT

All this was in his dreams; in real life, things were different. As an officer under Sulla, he had proven his valor. But he had won no fame, for Sulla did not share his glory with his lieutenants. As for the people, Crassus had won their friendship with his generosity, and they were willing to forget that he had served the dictator they hated. But he had not yet proved that in him was the heroic stuff of which great commanders—and rulers—are made.

Crassus' chance to be a hero came when

CRASSUS MADE A FORTUNE BY RUNNING THE FIRE DEPARTMENT IN ROME.

Spartacus, a gladiator, led a revolt of 90,000 runaway slaves. Spartacus' men were tough. Many of them were trained gladiators, and they had nothing more to lose than the lives they risked every day in the arenas. Others were savage tribesmen who had been captured in the border wars. For two years, the army of slaves kept to the mountains, raiding and robbing the cities below. As they moved north toward the Alps and freedom, more runaways came out of hiding to join them. They slaughtered every army sent against them. Realizing how strong his forces were, Spartacus wheeled them around and began to march toward Rome. The city, teeming with hundreds of thousands of restless slaves, had not faced such danger since the time of Hannibal. Crassus, given his first command of an army, crushed Spartacus' main force and drove the stragglers into the lines of a second Roman army, which finished them off. Crassus hurried home, expecting to be greeted as a hero. Instead, he watched while the general of the other army, Gnaeus Pompey, rode in a triumphal procession and took all the credit for breaking the rebellion.

Winning cheers as well as battles was Pompey's special talent. With his handsome face and proud bearing, he looked as a hero should look. People said he resembled the statues of Alexander. And, unlike Crassus, he had not let Sulla rob him of his fame. After his first successful campaign, in Africa, he had demanded a Triumph. When Sulla angrily refused, Pompey threatened to complain to the people and the army. "You know," he said, staring meaningfully at Sulla, "more people kneel to the rising sun than to the setting sun."

The aging dictator got the point, and let his dashing young officer have his Triumph. Pompey tried to make it even more impressive by harnessing a pair of elephants to his chariot. But the elephants could not squeeze through the city gates, and he was forced to enter Rome like any other conqueror, behind four horses. He made up for that when he was asked what name he wished to be given in honor of his victory. He chose to be called Pompey the Great.

"Great in comparison to what?" Crassus said when he heard the news. But Crassus' wealth, generosity, and victories were no match for Pom-

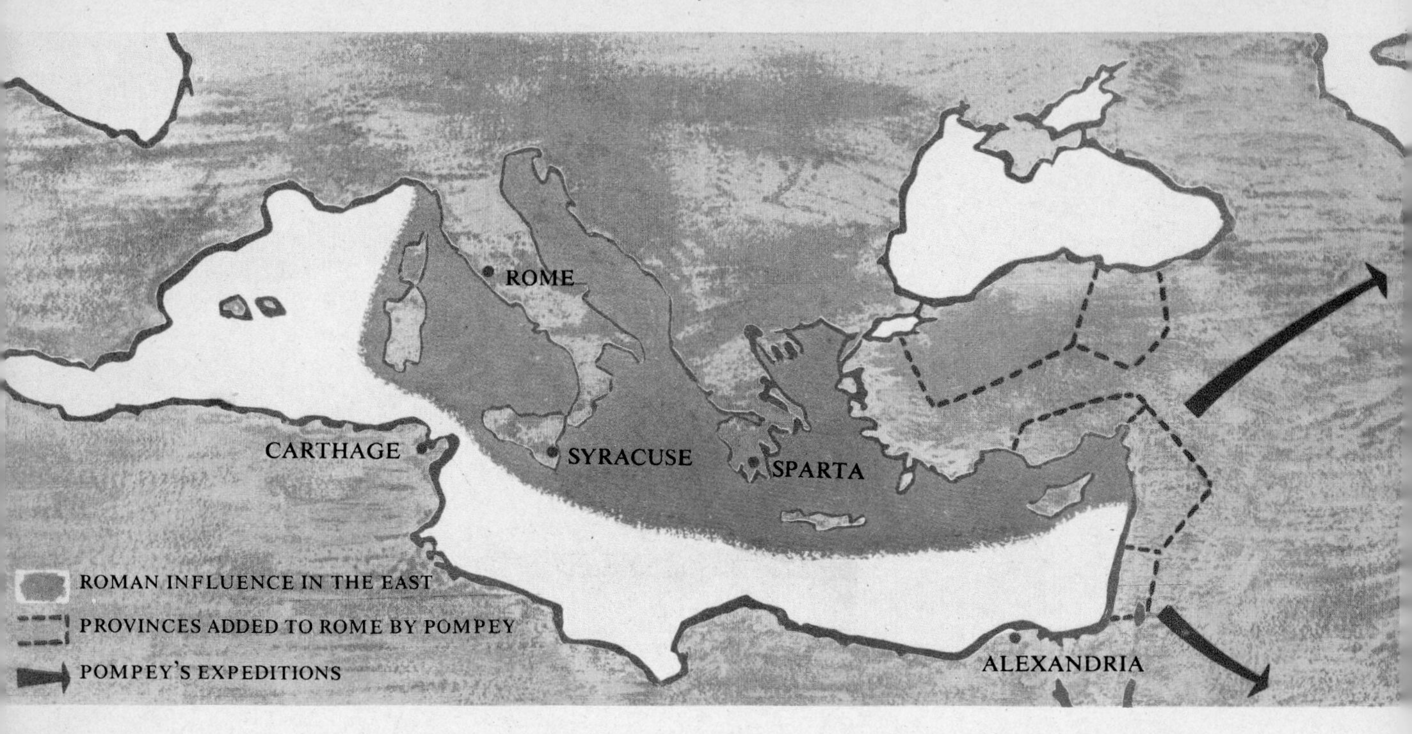

POMPEY'S CAMPAIGN IN ASIA MINOR REACHED AS FAR AS THE CASPIAN SEA.

pey's heroic appearance and manner. For a while, Crassus managed to keep up with his rival. After Sulla's death, both of them had joined the people's party and helped to destroy the new constitution which had been forced on Rome. Later, both were elected as consul-commanders, and both took care to show that the Senate could not order them around. But it was Pompey alone whom the citizens chose to lead a great expedition against the pirates who were robbing the Roman merchant fleet. While the senators shouted in anger, the people voted to give their favorite general a fleet of 500 ships. They put him in charge of the entire Mediterranean and all Roman land within fifty miles of its shores.

Luckily, Pompey was the right man for the job. The Mediterranean pirates were not little bands of ruffians. They sailed great fleets of stolen ships and preyed on the most important shipping routes. Their fortress-cities, tucked away among the islands in the Aegean Sea, were piled high with loot. Their dungeons were crowded with prisoners, waiting for their families to ransom them with gold. No merchant vessel or private yacht was safe from the sea raiders, and they had grown so bold that they dared to sail to the mouth of the Tiber, fifteen miles from Rome. But it took Pompey only forty days to sweep them out of the western half of the ocean. It took him only forty-nine days more to corner them in the Aegean, sink their ships, and destroy their island strongholds.

THE YOUNG JULIUS CAESAR

In Rome, the delighted people outshouted the Senate again and ordered Pompey to take command of Asia Minor. There he finished off Rome's old enemy, Mithridates. He took Judea and conquered the last of the Seleucids, the once-powerful kings who held the land that Alexander the Great had won in Asia. Then he led his legions along the Euphrates River all the way to the Caspian Sea. No one but Alexander had ever conquered so much of the Orient. When Pompey came home, he had won a huge new empire for Rome and treasure worth $36,000,000.

The triumphal procession lasted for two full days, and even Crassus admitted that Pompey deserved it. It was Pompey's third Triumph. The first had been for his conquests in Africa, the second for his conquests in Italy and Gaul, and now this one for his conquests in Asia. Taken together, they added up to most of the known world, all of it conquered for Rome by Pompey. Yet he did not try to be another Sulla. He disbanded his armies, and all that he asked the Romans was their agreement to the treaties he had made in the East and farmland for his soldiers. For two years the Senate ignored his requests. The senators had not forgiven the insult of the election which had given him his power. Pompey the Great was not their man and they were pleased to humble him.

Then another, younger officer, a leader of the people's party, offered his help to Pompey. He was Julius Caesar, and he came to Pompey with the idea for a partnership to rule Rome and the world. Young Caesar was a brilliant soldier, and even more eager to get ahead than Pompey or Crassus. It was said that when he first read about Alexander the Great, he cried. At his age Alexander had conquered so many nations, while he himself had done nothing worth remembering. But Alexander had not had Sulla as an enemy. Caesar was a nephew of Marius, and Sulla had kept a watchful eye on him. Although Caesar was then only a boy, his friends had had to talk fast to persuade Sulla not to kill him. Sulla had finally agreed, but he was certain he was making a mistake. "In that youngster," he said, "we have another Marius."

Sulla was wrong, for Caesar was not another Marius. He had none of his uncle's tough, peasant strength, and he had to train himself to stand up to the strain of battle. But Sulla was right when he said the boy was dangerous. Like Marius, he dreamed of commanding the legions, and he was much more clever than Marius had been. On the island of Rhodes, where he went to stay out of Sulla's way, he began to study at the school of Apollonius, a master in the Greek art of speech making. He learned the many ways to persuade a crowd, how to judge an opponent's weaknesses at a glance—all the tricks of city politics which had so baffled Marius. But there was no professor who could teach Caesar all he wanted to know. He taught himself, driving himself to read and think, just as he drove his body to make it strong. His textbooks were the speeches and histories of the great rulers of the world. It was not what they had done that interested him. He wanted to find out how they had managed to do it. How had they run their campaigns? How had they handled their soldiers? What did they say to the citizens they served, and the ones they conquered? As Caesar pored over his books, he learned to plan everything he did with the care and caution of a general preparing for a battle.

When Sulla died and the leaders of the people's party dared to show their faces in Rome again, Caesar went home. Now his family connection with Marius was an advantage. It made him something of a hero to the common citizens—at least, most of them knew his name. But Caesar was determined that before long they would know more about him than that.

Like Crassus, he set out to become the people's friend. With his charming manner and skill in making speeches, it was an easy job. Just as easily, he befriended Crassus himself. The millionaire was as worried as ever that the people would not like him enough. He was delighted to have the popular young nephew of Marius as his friend. As for Caesar, he had a plan of his own.

THE FIRST TRIUMVIRATE

In 68 B.C., Caesar won a post with the army in Spain, and soon the word spread that he was a daring officer, a man who deserved something better. When he returned to Rome, important men in the people's party began to say that he ought to run for office. Of course, that was just what he meant to do. But he was poor, and winning the support of the Romans cost money. When he was elected Aedile, the officer in charge of public celebrations, he treated the people to the most lavish shows they had ever seen. He staged great processions, gave public feasts, and once filled an arena with 320 pairs of gladiators. He became more popular than any other politician in the city, but he went far into debt. Crassus paid the bills—which had been Caesar's plan all along. It was money well spent, because Caesar soon won offices that brought him the riches to repay the loans. His popularity was as useful to Crassus as Crassus' money had been to him.

It was in 62 B.C. that Pompey the Great came home to two days of triumph and two years of snubs from the Senate. The conqueror of the world fumed while the senators, still trying to be the only rulers of Rome, ignored his requests. Then Caesar came up with a new plan. He discussed it first with Crassus, who was doubtful but did not say no. He talked to Pompey, who was interested if Crassus would agree. Caesar brought the two rivals together, trying to work out the details of a three-way partnership. That was a plan—a practical, Roman sort of plan, like his old arrangement with Crassus. Each of them wanted something, Caesar said. He himself wanted to be elected consul. Crassus hoped to see laws passed that would help his business friends, the knights. Pompey, of course, was worried about his treaties and the land for his soldiers. And each of them had something valuable to bring to the partnership. Caesar mentioned his own popularity. Crassus had money, and Pompey—Caesar smiled—Pompey was a hero. If Crassus and Pompey could forget their old rivalry, Caesar said, the partnership would be unbeatable.

Never had Caesar tried so hard to put Apollonius' arts of persuasion to work. As he spoke, Pompey began to see the end of his troubles with the Senate, and Crassus dreamed again of his great victory. Caesar's plan was too good to refuse. Pompey and Crassus agreed to end their rivalry, and swore eternal friendship to each other and to Caesar. The three shared a bowl of wine and drank to the success of the partnership. To seal the bargain, Caesar gave his young daughter in marriage to Pompey.

After that, it made little difference what the Senate did. Rome's future was no longer being settled in the Senate It was settled, secretly and unofficially, by the three men who gathered around the table in Crassus' dining room. In history, these three—Caesar, Pompey, and Crassus—would be known as the First Triumvirate. Their enemies called it the Three-headed Monster.

CAESAR'S WARS IN GAUL

In 59 B.C., Caesar was elected consul. Once he was in office, Pompey's treaties were made official, his soldiers were awarded their land, and Crassus' laws were passed. So far, the practical arrangement was working well. Then, the next year, Caesar was given a five-year command of the armies in Gaul. It was his chance to prove his brilliance as a commander, and he did. He crushed the fierce Gauls, pushing his armies across their lands as far as the English Channel and the Rhine River. After that, he crossed the channel and took almost half of Britain. The reports that came back from the front praised Caesar's strategy and the loyalty of his soldiers. They told of a commander who seemed never to sleep, who kept two secretaries busy at once taking down his orders for his captains. When a great revolt of the Gauls nearly destroyed his armies, he somehow held on and finally defeated the Gallic warriors.

Meanwhile, Pompey and Crassus sat impatiently in Rome. Not only were they still jealous of each other, they were now jealous of Caesar, too. The practical partnership was becoming a three-way rivalry. The senators, quick to take advantage of this, began to treat Pompey in a surprisingly friendly way. They hoped to win him to their side and break up the partnership.

Caesar called for a conference. The partners met and a new bargain was struck, one that gave each of them a command. They divided the world among themselves, like greedy schoolboys splitting up a pie. Gaul went to Caesar, Spain to Pompey, and Syria to Crassus. But, again like greedy boys, each began to wonder if his slice was as good or as big as the others, and each made his own, secret plan to take more than his fair share. While Pompey lingered in Rome, Caesar hurried back to Europe, where half a continent waited for anyone strong enough to take it away from the barbarians. Crassus put on his golden armor, collected an army of seven legions, and sailed to the East to be a hero at last. Pompey, however, delayed taking up his command in Spain. He remained in Rome, where he could strengthen his political position.

During the next three years, everything seemed to go wrong for the partnership. Crassus' expedition was plagued with problems. First there was the desert, a vast, hostile wasteland, where his army's scouts lost their bearings and the legions struggled on with never enough food or water. Then there was the enemy—a host of ruthless barbarians, old hands at desert warfare and burning with hate for the Romans who had killed their champion, Mithridates. And then there was Crassus himself.

His soldiers quickly realized that he was a bungler, a general who would waste their lives. They followed him because they had no choice. But they shambled along, grumbling, halfhearted, not knowing or caring where they were going, and expecting the worst. In 53 B.C., in the fiery heat of the Syrian summer, the worst happened. A horde of Asian lancers and mounted archers galloped out of the desert. While Crassus looked on in horror, the Asians surrounded his troops and savagely chopped them down. Twenty thousand of his men were killed, and 10,000 were taken prisoner. Crassus himself came out of the

POMPEY THE GREAT

JULIUS CAESAR

battle alive. But afterwards, when he went to what he thought would be a truce conference, the barbarians murdered him. They stripped the splendid armor from his body and cut off his head as a prize for their king—a nightmare ending to the dreams of the richest man in Rome.

THE STRUGGLE FOR POWER

And now there were only two partners to divide the world between them. Caesar and his veterans were still in Europe. Pompey was still in Rome. He never went to Spain; there were more important campaigns to be waged in the capital. The city was in a turmoil. The Senate, as always, claimed the right to run the Republic, but outside the Senate house, the streets were ruled by gangs of thugs. One gang, led by Clodius, a renegade officer, looked out for Caesar's interests in Rome. Another, Milo's gang, worked for Pompey. They used their fists to win votes and their swords to silence speakers who took the wrong side in an argument. When Milo's men murdered Clodius, gang wars broke out. The senators asked Pompey to round up the toughs with his troops. They suggested that the job of keeping the peace might be easier if Rome had only one consul instead of the usual two. The one, of course, would be Pompey—if he cooperated with the Senate.

It was a tempting offer, the whole pie instead of half. It would mean betraying Caesar and breaking the partnership. But, after all, Crassus was dead. Pompey's wife had died, too, and his friendship for her father had died with her. Why shouldn't he be the only consul in Rome? For the hero who had conquered the world and resembled Alexander, it was only right. Or so the senators said, and Pompey, who was never a man to underrate himself, agreed. So Pompey became the Senate's man, and its defender against Caesar. Now the political battle between the people's party and the aristocrats was a contest between two generals, a dispute that could only be settled on the battlefield.

Caesar, sure of the loyalty of his veterans, continued campaigning. The book he wrote about his wars and victories in Gaul made certain that the Romans knew just how much he was doing for them. Meanwhile, Pompey happily took on the job of ruling Rome, and tried to win the people's thanks in his own way. He put bigger, wilder shows in the arenas. He built a new theater, the first stone theater in the city. He opened a splendid public garden inside a square of fine new buildings. On one side of the square, he built a meeting-hall, the Curia, where he and the Senate could discuss the business of Rome in comfort. A feature of the new hall was a statue of Pompey the Great, bigger than life and looking very much like Alexander.

In 49 B.C., the former partners, now enemies, faced each other again. Caesar had been given his command in Gaul for five years, and the time was up. The Senate ordered him to come home—without his soldiers. Caesar replied with an offer to disband his army if Pompey would do the same. While he waited for an answer, he marched his army to the Rubicon, the river that marked the boundary between Gaul and Italy. On his side of the river, Caesar was the consul-commander of Gaul, with the right to have an army. On the other side, in Italy, he had no lawful powers at all; he was just another Roman citizen. If he crossed the Rubicon at the head of an army, the law would say that he was an invader, an enemy of the Republic, the Senate, and Pompey.

Speeding from Rome came the messengers, among them Caesar's lieutenant, Mark Antony. Caesar's offer had been refused, he said. The Senate commanded him to disband his legions or be declared a public enemy. Caesar nodded grimly. Then he signaled to his captains and led the army across the river. When he reached Rome, Pompey and most of the senators were gone. They had no army to equal Caesar's and they had fled to Greece. Caesar moved swiftly. He stayed in the city only long enough for the people to elect him consul-commander. Then, as the legal leader of the Roman armies, no longer an invader or an outlaw, he took his troops to Spain and defeated Pompey's allies there.

THE END OF POMPEY

Meanwhile, Pompey raised an army and prepared to invade Italy. But before he could sail, Caesar rushed to Greece to stop him. At Pharsalus in Thessaly, the old partners met on the battlefield. Pompey had nine Roman legions and a great force of Greek and Macedonian horsemen, the best cavalrymen in the world. Caesar had his veteran infantrymen, a few battalions of men Mark Antony had rounded up in Italy, and no cavalry at all. Pompey attacked. His horsemen charged across the plain, crashing against a wall of Caesar's footsoldiers. The tough infantrymen, veterans of countless fights against the barbarians, held their ground. They hauled at the horses, pulling them around so that they could attack the riders. By afternoon, they had killed or wounded so many men that the armies were now evenly matched. They began to push across the plain. Pompey's legions fell back, broke their lines, and ran for their lives. And still the infantry pushed ahead, to the edge of the plain, and beyond to the enemy camp.

After the battle, Pompey the Great walked from the field in silence. He spoke only once, when he saw Caesar's soldiers trailing his men to their tents. "In the very camp?" he cried, and was silent again. He escaped to a ship, sailed across the Mediterranean, and anchored just off the coast of Egypt. He sent a message to the young King Ptolemy, begging for a place of refuge in his court. Then he waited while the king made up his mind. When, finally, an ordinary rowboat was sent to pick him up, Pompey knew that Ptolemy did not intend to welcome him with honor. But he boarded the boat and, on the way to the shore, he studied a little speech he had written in Greek, his humble greeting to his new protector. Near the beach, his servant leaped out of the boat to help him ashore. As Pompey began to stand up, one of the Egyptian sailors stabbed him from behind—the king had decided that he would be a dangerous guest. The sailors hauled him out of the boat, cut off his head as proof to the king that he was dead, and left his body on the beach. Later, when the Egyptians had gone away, Pompey's servant found a battered fishing boat half buried in the sand, and he used it to make a funeral pyre for his master. It was a lonely end for a hero who had always had a crowd to cheer him.

So, of the three partners, only Caesar was left. In the spring of 48 B.C., the Roman world belonged to him. By autumn of the same year, he had almost lost it, along with his life. The trouble came when he went to Egypt looking for Pompey, not knowing that Pompey was already dead. He found himself caught in the middle of a royal family quarrel. Ptolemy, the thirteen-year-old king of Egypt, shared his throne with his sister, Cleopatra, who was twenty. But sharing the throne in this way was an Egyptian custom, not something that either of them wanted. They were clever but spoiled children, and jealous of each other. They constantly bickered and threw the court into an uproar with their tantrums. Then they began to plot against each other, until their feuding became the talk of Alexandria. The people took the side of the little king. When Cleopatra showed her temper once too often, a group of citizens escorted her out of the city and told her not to come back. This happened just at the time that Caesar arrived in Egypt.

CAESAR AND CLEOPATRA

Cleopatra had heard about Julius Caesar, and she knew that he was the most powerful man in Rome. She arranged to meet him, and found that he was a pleasant man. He was not as young as he might have been, perhaps, but he was courtly and polite. And, of course, he was a very great general.

Cleopatra said she was helpless to defend herself. She needed someone strong to look after her—someone like Caesar. She was a beautiful woman, and knew how to handle men. Caesar was charmed, and then conquered completely. He promised to do what he could. He marched into Alexandria, captured the palace, made Ptolemy his prisoner, and handed over the throne to the beautiful queen.

The Alexandrians were not pleased. They called out the army of Egypt and attacked the palace. This was more than Caesar had bargained for; he had come to Egypt with very few soldiers. For six months, it was all he could do to hold the palace. In the spring of 47 B.C., he let Ptolemy go free, hoping that the Alexandrians would call off their troops. Instead, they rallied around the young king, attacking Caesar and Cleopatra more fiercely than ever. The conqueror of Pompey and the Gauls stood a good chance of being killed in this little Egyptian squabble. Then, just in time, reinforcements galloped in from Asia Minor and saved him. With their help, Caesar took control of Alexandria, killed Ptolemy, and chased the Egyptian army around the desert until he was certain that no one would try to steal Cleopatra's throne again.

BY CROSSING THE RUBICON WITH HIS LEGIONS, CAESAR CHALLENGED THE SENATE.

By then, it was autumn, and Caesar had stayed in Egypt much longer than he had planned. He learned that the barbarians who had defeated Crassus were invading Rome's provinces in Asia, and Pompey's sons had taken Africa for the Senate. Yet whenever Caesar thought of leaving Cleopatra, he found some reason to stay, and he remained in Egypt throughout the winter.

TRIUMPH AND DEATH

When spring came, and good campaigning weather, he at last said good-by to Egypt and its queen. He formed his legions and marched into Asia to try to repair the damage which Crassus had done. He wasted no time about it. By September he had fought and won forty-seven battles and was on the way to Africa. The fighting was rougher there, the victories came slowly, but in the summer of 46 B.C., he destroyed the last of the senators' armies. Then he returned to Rome.

His parade of triumph was as splendid as any the old city had ever seen. It marked not one but four great conquests—his victories over Gaul, Africa, Egypt, and Asia. On one of the chariots that led the long procession, three words were painted: *Veni, vidi, vici*—"I came, I saw, I conquered." That was the message Caesar had sent to Rome after his campaign in Asia. Now, as the chariot rolled along the street, people shouted, "*Veni, vidi, vici!*" The throngs took up the shout until it echoed across the city. When Caesar himself rode by, dressed in his purple robe and carrying the laurel branch of victory, the thunderous shouting seemed to shake the hills of Rome. *Veni, vidi, vici!* The conqueror of the world, the champion of the people, had come home at last.

Caesar had great plans for Rome—plans for roads, plans for buildings, plans for colonies, plans for new campaigns. He would make certain that his soldiers had a fair share of the land they had fought for, and that the poor of the city had food. He would send honest governors to the provinces. And he himself would govern with justice, not murder. He did everything he could to show Romans that he was not like Sulla or Marius. Instead of killing the men who had worked against him, he pardoned them. He declared himself dictator of Rome for life, with the consent of the Senate and the people. It was true that no one dared to vote against this. But twice, when the mob offered him the crown of a king, he refused it. He was satisfied to be dictator; he would not destroy the Republic by becoming king.

Many of the senators came over to Caesar's side. Others, however, did not trust him. Caesar was hungry for power, they said. Already he had made himself dictator. If a crown was offered to him a third time, they asked, would he refuse it again?

The most determined of Caesar's enemies in the Senate was Gaius Cassius, who hoped to stir up a plot against him. But Cassius was an old officer of Pompey's and spiteful as well; few men were willing to follow him. A very different sort of person was Senator Marcus Junius Brutus. He came from one of the oldest, most respected families in Rome. He was Caesar's friend, and he had served with him in the great campaigns in Asia. Everyone knew Brutus as a thoughtful, honest man. When Cassius came to him with his whining complaints about Caesar, Brutus at first refused to listen. But Cassius came again with new arguments. He said that all of Rome remembered Brutus' ancestors, because they had led the fight to drive the old Etruscan kings from Rome. Brutus nodded. Driving out the tyrants was the proudest event in the long history of his family. "And now," Cassius said, "will Brutus stand by, doing nothing while a new tyrant robs the Romans of their freedom?"

Brutus made no answer, but Cassius knew that he had won his point. He gave Brutus time to weigh his love for his friend Caesar against the freedom of Rome and family duty. As he expected, Brutus at last agreed to join the plot. After that, persuading the others was easy. Men who had been suspicious of Cassius were willing to follow honest Brutus. Soon, more than twenty senators had joined the conspiracy and sworn to stop the power-hungry Caesar before it was too late.

On the morning of March 15, 44 B.C., Caesar was getting ready to attend a meeting of the Senate when his wife Calpurnia rushed into the room. Her hair was flying and uncombed, and tears ran down her face. She had had a terrible dream, she said. All through the night she had dreamed of death and of danger to Caesar. She begged him to stay home and not go to the Senate. Caesar laughed and shook his head. The dictator of Rome, the commander-in-chief of the armies, could not give up important state business because his wife had had a nightmare.

A BAND LED BY CASSIUS AND BRUTUS STABBED CAESAR AT THE SENATE.

Calpurnia begged him again. She said she knew that it was more than a nightmare; it was a sign from the gods. She reminded Caesar that a soothsayer had warned him to beware of this day, the fifteenth, which was called the Ides of March. When Caesar saw how terrified his wife was, he asked his priests to sacrifice an animal and study it for omens. A favorable report from the priests would calm Calpurnia's fears, and, in fact, Caesar himself wanted to be told that all was well. But the report was far from comforting. The omens were bad, the priests said, very bad indeed.

Like every Roman, Caesar knew that it was dangerous to ignore that sort of warning. When his friend Mark Antony came to walk with him to the Senate, he told him to go on alone and to dismiss the meeting. But another friend, a senator, urged Caesar not to insult the Senate so, especially on a day when they were going to discuss making him a king over the provinces. Once more, Caesar changed his mind. He would go to the Senate. When Calpurnia shrieked and the priests began to chatter at him, he silenced them with one sentence: "The omens," he said, "shall be what Caesar makes them be."

As he walked through the city, nothing seemed different or out of the ordinary. The streets were busy, as usual. The same crowds gave him the same cheers. Once a man darted out, thrust a note into Caesar's hand, and disappeared into the throng as though he did not want to be seen. Caesar started to look at the note, but someone spoke to him and he forgot about it. Near the Senate, the Curia which Pompey had built, he heard a man call out to him. It was the soothsayer, and Caesar smiled when he saw him. "The Ides of March are come," he said.

"Yes," the soothsayer answered, "but they are not past."

Caesar smiled again and started up the steps of the Curia. Inside, a group of senators was waiting to speak to him. One of them walked up to him and asked a question. As Caesar turned to answer, the man pulled a dagger from the folds of his toga and stabbed him. Then the other senators in the group—Cassius and Brutus and the rest—crowded around him. Each of them had a dagger. Caesar glared at them, his eyes going from face to face, until he recognized Brutus, who had been his friend. *"Et tu, Brute?"* he cried. "You too, Brutus?" Then he covered his eyes with his toga and let the daggers strike. When the assassins drew back, he crumpled to the floor, just at the foot of the tall statue of Pompey.

Caesar, the last of the three partners, was dead.

YOUNG OCTAVIUS WAS THE NEPHEW AND HEIR TO THE POWER OF JULIUS CAESAR.

The Second Triumvirate

43 B.C.-30 B.C.

As THE news of Caesar's death spread through Rome, sorrow and anger and fear took hold of the city. On March 17, two days after the murder, the Senate met again. Cassius, Brutus, and the other assassins took their usual places. There was no doubt that most of their fellow senators felt that they had done the right thing in ridding Rome of a tyrant. But Caesar's veterans were still in the city, taking their orders now from Marcus Aemilius Lepidus, who had been his Master of the Horse, the commander of the cavalry. Mark Antony was still consul, he had not yet said what he intended to do about Caesar's murder, but certainly he would not forgive the killers. And, of course, no one could tell what the mob might do. If the people took it into their heads to avenge the murder of their hero, there might be many more killings. So it was a cautious, quiet group of men who gathered in the Senate to discuss the death of Caesar and the future of Rome.

When Mark Antony spoke, he surprised them by not demanding that the assassins be arrested and put on trial. Perhaps he was afraid that they had strong forces of their own or that he might be the next victim. Whatever his reasons were, he offered to make a bargain. He would agree to let the assassins go unpunished, if the Senate would agree to approve Caesar's will and allow his friends to give him a proper, public funeral. To the senators, the terms sounded fair—better, in fact, than they had hoped for. They quickly agreed to their part of the bargain, ended the meeting, and went home, congratulating themselves that it all had been so easy.

THE FUNERAL OF CAESAR

On the day of the funeral, a restless crowd packed the Forum. Caesar's body was carried into the square at the head of a great procession. The long columns of his soldiers filed past, and the city officers, and his friends, who had dressed themselves in the splendid purple gowns which he had worn in his parades of triumph. Carried high, so that everyone could see it, was an ivory couch on which was spread the robe which Caesar wore that last morning at the Senate house. The cloth was bloodstained and marked with the twenty-three slashes made by the daggers of his killers.

When the procession stopped in the Forum, Mark Antony began to speak to the crowd about Caesar, his friend. He read aloud from Caesar's will. It said that his gardens along the River Tiber should be opened to the public as a park, and that every Roman citizen should be given a sum of money from his fortune—300 sesterces, about 15 dollars. A murmur of pleased surprise swept through the crowd, but it soon gave way to angry shouts of "Death to the murderers!" Antony spoke on, for he had more to say about Caesar's generosity. But suddenly his speech was interrupted. Someone in the crowd threw a torch onto the couch on which the body lay. As the couch began to burn, more torches were thrown. A kind of madness, partly grief and partly wild excitement, seized the people in the Forum. Caesar's friends tore off their purple robes and threw them into the flames. Women flung their jewelry, and soldiers added their banners. Then a man took a branch from the fire, brandished it over his head, and called for everyone who had loved Caesar to follow him to the houses of the murderers. The fury of the crowd broke loose. They poured from the Forum into the streets, shouting and waving torches. Behind them, Mark Antony stood silently smiling, while the flames of the funeral pyre flickered and blazed higher.

Caesar's veterans still guarded the peace of Rome, so the assassins' homes were not burned. But the soldiers had no commander in chief and Rome was without a ruler. The days that followed the funeral brought confusion and civil war, while the Romans struggled to find a man or a government that could bring order to the world which they had conquered.

Cassius and Brutus said that they had killed Caesar to save the Republic. But the Republic had long been dead. It had been killed by Sulla, and Marius, and the senators who were greedy, and the people who could only be trusted when a man with an army told them what to do. The senators tried to take control of the state, but Mark Antony had already turned their old enemy, the mob, against them and their new leaders. Soon Cassius and Brutus had to flee from the city, leaving Cicero to guide the Senate with his artfully made speeches. But Cicero knew politics in Rome too well to believe that fine words in the Senate could control the Romans. He knew that the Senate needed a champion to fight for it, another Sulla or another Pompey, if it was ever to have its way again. Like Caesar's soldiers and all of Rome, he waited for the new commander to appear.

OCTAVIUS COMES TO ROME

Mark Antony, of course, hoped to be the new Caesar. His speech at the funeral, and the riot it stirred up, had been carefully planned as the first step in his campaign. But in the will, which he had shown so openly to the crowd in the Forum, Caesar himself had named an heir. He had not chosen Mark Antony. Instead, he had given his titles, his fortune, and his place in Rome to his nephew, Caesar Octavius.

Octavius was just eighteen, a student in Greece. Antony and other men in Rome sent him messages urging him to stay away from the city. His life would be in danger, they said, and there was little he could do in Rome without Caesar to protect him. But Octavius decided that he might be able to do a great deal more than they expected. If he was Caesar's heir, then he would act like Caesar. He ignored the warnings and rushed to Rome to claim what was rightfully his.

Mark Antony tried to greet Octavius as though he was glad to see him, but he found it hard to do. The young man seemed too much like a rival. He was handsome. He had his uncle's talent for charming the people. And, like Caesar, he dealt ruthlessly with anyone who got in his way. When Antony came to greet him, Octavius was polite but cold. He was angered by Antony's attempts to talk to him like a jolly older brother, and was not frightened by Antony's threats. He reminded Antony sharply that he, Caesar Octavius, was Caesar's only heir, and he did not mean to share his inheritance.

Antony left him alone then. He was annoyed that the young man was so stubborn, but he was not greatly worried. After all, he thought, Octavius was little more than a child, with no army and no powerful friends in Rome. He might be a bother, but nothing more.

But Cicero, the crafty leader of the Senate, had other ideas. He knew as much as any man could about the strange turnings and sudden shifts of power in Rome. From his place in the Senate house, he had watched the champions come and go. He had seen the strong ones honored, and the weak ones crushed and forgotten. But always, he himself came through safely, like a skillfully steered ship riding out a storm. He had grown up in Sulla's Senate and helped to snub Pompey when he came home from Asia. The Three-headed Monster had chased him out of Rome for a year or two, but in time the partners had invited him to come back. He had helped to persuade Pompey to fight for the Senate, yet Caesar had treated him with honor and asked his help in dealing with the politicians. When

CLEOPATRA WENT TO HER MEETING WITH MARK ANTONY ON HER LUXURIOUS BARGE.

Cicero thought of his long, successful career, he had every reason to be proud and pleased with himself. He had had many years of power, simply because he was clever. He had not joined the plot against Caesar; murder was not his way to solve a problem. But now that Caesar was dead, he was eagerly looking for a way to turn the turmoil in Rome into a victory for himself and the Senate. In the young Octavius, he saw a champion who seemed to fit into his scheme perfectly.

OCTAVIUS AND ANTONY

At first, Cicero said nothing. Meanwhile, he kept a sharp eye on Octavius. He was pleased to see how neatly the boy went about winning the mob to his side. Octavius discovered that Antony, the "guardian" of Caesar's fortune, had spent the money that was supposed to go to the people. When Antony refused to pay it back, Octavius began to sell his own possessions and to borrow in order to raise the money. Of course, when the gold was handed out, he made certain that everyone knew exactly what had happened. The stories of his generosity and honesty spread to the soldiers, the armies which gave Antony his power. Quietly the legions began to offer their services to Octavius, and Cicero decided that it was time for him to act. He went to Octavius and asked him to become the defender of Rome against Antony. He said that Octavius, with his popularity and the support of the soldiers, could easily take control of the city. Cicero promised that the Senate would make it legal.

Then, when Octavius had raised an army and Rome was again safe for the Senate, Cicero had no more use for him. "The young man is to be honored, to be praised, and to be pushed aside," he said. Once again the Senate would rule Rome.

With these words, Cicero condemned himself to death. For the young man would not be pushed aside. He marched his army against Rome instead of Antony. When he had captured the city, the people elected him consul. The election made Octavius the master of Rome and Italy. The provinces, however, were held by his rivals and enemies. Antony and Lepidus had taken the West. In the East, Brutus and Cassius had built a mammoth army. Octavius could not take on all of them at once. So he did what his uncle Caesar would have done: he invited his rivals to be his partners in a war against his enemies. He had no trouble persuading Antony and Lepidus to join him. And, in 42 B.C., the three of them were elected "Triumvirs of Rome," whose duty it was to hunt down and destroy the murderers of Caesar.

At Philippi, in Macedonia, Octavius and Antony each fought and won a battle against the armies of the assassins. Brutus and Cassius killed themselves to avoid capture. In Rome, Cicero was condemned and executed. Once again, the Roman world was in the hands of three greedy partners.

This Second Triumvirate was no secret, of course. It was the legal government of Rome, but it worked no better than the old partnership of Caesar, Crassus, and Pompey. Lepidus was weak. Antony and Octavius were rivals. When Antony went to campaign in Asia, he left his secret agents behind to stir up trouble in Italy, where Octavius was in charge. Octavius, in turn, cut

off Antony's supply of men and equipment. And the East was Antony's downfall, for it was there that he met Cleopatra, whose beauty had kept Caesar in Egypt for more than a year.

Cleopatra still dreamed of a Roman conqueror who could make her the Queen of the East or even of the Mediterranean. Caesar, her first choice, was dead. She had considered Pompey's son but he did not have enough power. Antony was a genuine conqueror with a strong army, and Cleopatra had heard that he had a weakness for beautiful women.

ANTONY AND CLEOPATRA

When he came to the East, soon after his victory at Philippi, Antony invited Cleopatra to visit him. The invitation was a matter of courtesy, for Egypt was an independent kingdom—Caesar had not insulted the queen by making her country a province. Cleopatra was delighted to have a chance to meet the great new general, but she did not answer his polite letter. She meant her arrival to be a surprise, one that she hoped he would not soon forget. Years later, the world still remembered every detail of what turned out to be one of the most important meetings in history. Plutarch, the famous Roman historian, heard about it from his grandfather, who had talked to a man who said he had been on the scene. Plutarch described it this way:

> *Cleopatra came sailing up the river in a barge with a gilded hull and outspread sails of purple, while oars of silver beat time to the music of flutes and fifes and harps. She herself lay under a canopy of gold, dressed like Venus, and beautiful children, like painted Cupids, stood on each side to fan her. Her maids were dressed as sea nymphs. Some of them stood steering at the rudder and others worked the sail-ropes while the sweet scent of perfumes drifted from the boat to the shore.*

Antony, the conqueror, was quickly conquered. Before long, he lost his interest in campaigning and hurried off to Alexandria and Cleopatra. He was like a schoolboy on vacation; he had no time for anything but pleasure. And Cleopatra was always at his side. She feasted with him, went hunting with him, and learned to play at dice

with him like a soldier. When he exercised his horse or practiced swordsmanship, she was there to watch. In the evenings, they rambled about Alexandria, dressed like beggars, bursting into the houses of astounded commoners or playing tricks on their own courtiers.

But, like all vacations, Antony's vacation came to an end. New wars broke out in Asia, and when Antony asked for troops from Rome, Octavius did not send them. Antony rushed home. A conference of the triumvirs was called, and, like the earlier partners, the three generals agreed to split the world among themselves. Octavius was to have Italy and the West, Antony was to have the East, and Lepidus was to have Africa, the thinnest slice of the pie. Again, a marriage sealed the bargain. When Antony returned to the East, he had a wife, Octavia, the sister of Octavius.

For two years Antony ruled Rome's eastern provinces from Athens, with Octavia at his side. Then troubling reports began to come to Rome. Octavius had taken over Lepidus' legions, thus doubling his power to twenty-two legions. He was master of the West and his successes were the talk of Rome.

Although Octavia did her best to keep peace between her husband and her brother, Antony insisted that he must do something to add to his reputation before the Romans forgot about him. He hurried to Asia to fight barbarians, and, he hoped, to win land and treasure. But the campaign did not go well. Although Antony lost no battles, he won no great victories, and many of his men were killed. Weary and discouraged, he went again to Egypt where life was pleasant. This time he stayed. When Octavia wrote to ask if she should come to Alexandria, he told her to go back to Rome.

OCTAVIUS WON MASTERY OVER ANTONY IN THE GREAT SEA BATTLE OF ACTIUM.

Cleopatra was full of plans for Antony and herself. Soon both of them were talking about the world which they would rule together. They were married, despite Octavia, who still waited in Italy. Then Cleopatra crowned Antony as her king, and she spoke as though their kingdom would include a number of cities which belonged to the Romans. When the news reached Italy, Octavius ended the partnership and the Senate declared Antony the enemy of Rome.

THE BATTLE OF ACTIUM

In 31 B.C., the forces of the two partners met in a great sea battle near Actium in Greece. The sides were almost even; each commander had come with 500 warships and more than 40,000 legionaries. But Antony's crews, Romans who found themselves fighting for Egypt, had been told wild, frightening tales about Cleopatra's ambition to rule the East. They had seen for themselves the strange ways of the Egyptians, and they half believed that Antony had been bewitched. When the battle began, many of them refused to fight. Cleopatra and her squadron were forced to break through a line of Octavius' battleships to avoid being captured. Antony, too, had to run from the fight, leaving most of his fleet to surrender or be taken.

In the morning, before the battle, Octavius had prayed to Apollo, promising to build him a new temple if he helped Rome to win a victory. By afternoon, Octavius knew that it would have to be a fine temple, for the victory was his, his losses were small, and his enemies had been badly beaten.

Antony and Cleopatra fled to Alexandria. In the summer of 30 B.C., Octavius marched his armies around the Aegean, through Asia Minor, and into Egypt. Antony tried to hold them off, but his men deserted as soon as the Roman standards came into sight. Then someone told him that Cleopatra was dead. He left the battlefield, found a quiet place, and killed himself.

The story of Cleopatra's death was false, however. She was alive, waiting in Alexandria for Antony—or perhaps Octavius. When the city was taken, she was made a captive in her own splendid palace. Octavius, the new Caesar, came once to visit her, but her charms did not seem to affect him. Then she learned that he planned to take her to Rome in chains, like any other prisoner of war. She called for her priests to bring her an asp, a poisonous snake that was sacred to her goddess Isis. She said farewell to her maids, let the asp bite her, and in a moment she was dead.

Now Egypt belonged to Octavius, and so did all the Roman world. It was a tired, confused world, longing for peace. For too many years it had been the battlefield on which Romans slaughtered other Romans.

The new master of Rome was thirty-two years old. Perhaps it was good that he was young, because making peace would be much more difficult than making war had been, and it would take time.

OCTAVIUS CAESAR BECAME AUGUSTUS, A NAME GRANTED EARLIER ONLY TO GODS.

The City of Augustus

29 B.C.-A.D. 14

IN 29 B.C. the gates of war were closed. Rome was at peace.

Senators and the people of the mob—men who had hated and fought each other through long, bitter years—stood side by side in the Forum while the great doors of the temple of Janus were slowly pushed shut. That had happened only twice before in the history of the city.

The crowd in the Forum cheered the peace, and they cheered Octavius, their new ruler. He was no longer the young man who had rushed to Rome after the murder of his uncle, Caesar. Seventeen years had passed since then—seventeen years of hard campaigning, of friends who became enemies, and of alliances that were broken. He was still handsome, and his sharp eyes could still look through a man. But he walked with a new dignity that won him the respect of the people and Senate alike. Wherever he went, cheering crowds followed him. His friends told him that he could make himself the king of Rome. But Octavius remembered what had happened when Caesar had thought of becoming a king.

Caesar had proved that one man with an army could do what the bickering Senate and the mob could not do: he could run the empire. A world with millions of people in it was still like the smallest Roman family; it worked best with only one *pater familias*. Octavius meant to be that all-powerful father of Rome, but he intended to let the Romans think that they had asked him to be it.

He celebrated his Triumph with processions that went on for three days. With the treasures he had won in Egypt, he bought land to give to his soldiers. He ordered the building of a splendid temple to Apollo, as he had vowed he would before the battle at Actium. Then he gave up all his powers as a military commander and officer of the state. "Once more the laws of Rome are in the hands of the people and the senate," he said.

The Senate, however, rushed to ask him if he would not, at least, accept the command of Gaul, Spain, and Syria. He did, and that put him in charge of nearly all the legions. In gratitude, the Senate gave him a laurel wreath for saving the lives of citizens, a golden shield, and the new name Augustus. It was a name of honor that had been given only to gods before. But in the eyes of Rome, this man who had brought peace was a god. Then the Senate elected him *princeps.* It was a new office, and the name meant "the first"—the first citizen of Rome. Years later, the word came to be "prince," for that is what Augustus made it mean.

AUGUSTUS REBUILDS ROME

By their votes, the Romans had made Augustus more powerful than any king had ever been, but he was careful not to act like a king. He kept the old custom of wearing only clothes made in his own household. He lived in a house that was smaller and less elegant than the homes of many of his citizens. He made a great show of consulting the Senate before announcing any decision. Elections were still held to name consuls, tribunes, and the rest, though somehow Augustus' men always won and often he was elected to one or more of these posts himself.

He was just as careful to see that nearly everyone had something to be grateful for and little to complain about. His soldiers' pay was good and they could look forward to gifts of land when they were mustered out. The knights, his businessmen, were making money faster than ever before. The senators were happy with jobs in the provincial governments and appointments to the highway commission, the grain council, or one of the other committees he had started. The mob was well fed and too busy to make trouble.

Keeping the mob busy meant giving free shows. Augustus, usually a cautious spender, paid out vast sums of money for the people's entertainment. Ten thousand gladiators fought in the arenas during his reign, and he presented twenty-six wild-beast hunts in which 3,500 animals were killed. Each show went on for several days, and in one year, any Roman who had the stomach for it could have spent as many as 117 days in the grandstands of the arenas. But Augustus' greatest show was so enormous that no stadium in Rome was big enough to hold it. The stage was a gigantic pond, which he commanded to be dug in a field outside the city. Thirty warships were hauled to the pond, and 3,000 prisoners manned them and fought a naval battle for the amusement of the Romans. No one but Caesar had done anything like that before. And no one but Caesar had dreamed of changing the look of Rome as Augustus did.

The temple of Apollo was only the first of his projects. He built it entirely of the finest marble. And, because Apollo was the bringer of light and knowledge, Augustus had two libraries built beside its entrance—one for books in Greek, one for books in Latin. Then he began to repair and improve all the temples in Rome. More than eighty of the old shrines were rebuilt, and they glistened with new marble and fresh stucco. A series of great new buildings rose on the Campus Martius. One was a splendid temple for the gods of the stars and planets—the Pantheon. The old Forum was refurbished, and two new market places were built, the Forum of Julius and the Forum of Augustus. Wherever the Romans looked, there was another building crew at work. They began to say that Augustus had found a city of brick and made it a city of marble.

The new buildings were only one sign of the changes in Rome. Peace had increased trade, and the city was rich. Ships and long caravans of mules and camels came to Italy loaded with cloth, spices, fine furniture, silver vases, and dishes of gold. The ships brought people, too. Freemen from all the provinces poured into the city, looking for work and places to live. Tenements of brick and wood were hastily put up along already overcrowded streets. Rome was booming, and all the old problems of big cities—traffic and fire and crime—were worse than ever. But Augustus solved them. For the first time Rome had a police force to keep order in its streets and a fire department that did not belong to a Crassus.

THE NEW RICH

He was less successful when he tried to curb the wild spending in his city. Augustus firmly believed that the old-fashioned Roman way was the best way. A man lived simply, because luxuries would make him soft, and his money was something he put to work. But times had changed, and the Romans did not agree with Augustus. Never had there been so much money, and never had people

ROMAN BANQUETS BECAME LONG AND EXPENSIVE AFFAIRS.

worked so hard to spend it where it would show. Gone were the old noble families whose strict codes and plain living had built the Republic. Instead, men won fame with their riches. The city honored them, artists tried to please them, and poets flattered them, even though they might laugh at their extravagance behind their backs.

A huge house in town was no longer enough. By Caesar's time, anyone who was at all important had to have a *villa,* a sprawling estate in the country. In those days, Cicero, whose fine letters were filled with reports and gossip about the great men of his era, wrote about his brother's country house, a place which Cicero said was worthy of a Caesar. It had a sunny promenade and a colonnade for strolling, an aviary filled with rare birds, a wrestling ground, a fish pond, and a garden dotted with ivy-covered Greek statues.

STATUES AND BANQUETS

Cicero did not live to see the merchants who became millionaires soon after Octavius became Augustus. All of them wanted to live like Caesars. Suddenly, men who had longed for years to be important could afford to buy a place among the aristocrats and the great men who had ignored them—and they wanted the world to know it. Recklessly they poured out money for big houses, for draperies of Tyrian purple, for ivory couches and golden vases, and for genuine Greek statues. It did not really matter to them that many of these statues were only copies. The marble was Greek; so were the designs and the names of the artists. It was said that every Greek who could lift a hammer had turned into a sculptor. Those who did not copy statues specialized in carving stone portraits of citizens and their wives. With eyes as sharp as their chisels, they copied every line and bump of a face. But their clients never complained —if a man was a Roman, he had no need to be handsome.

The sculptors kept shop in little stalls along Rome's miles of colonnades, beside the Indian jewelers, who did a rushing business in diamonds, rubies, and pearls. There, too, were the food merchants, who searched the world for new delicacies rare and expensive enough to suit the tastes of the people who gave banquets to impress their friends. Roast peacock, presented to the diners on a silver tray decorated with its tailfeathers, was a common dish. So was the whole roast boar, carried in from the kitchen by four or five slaves. An im-

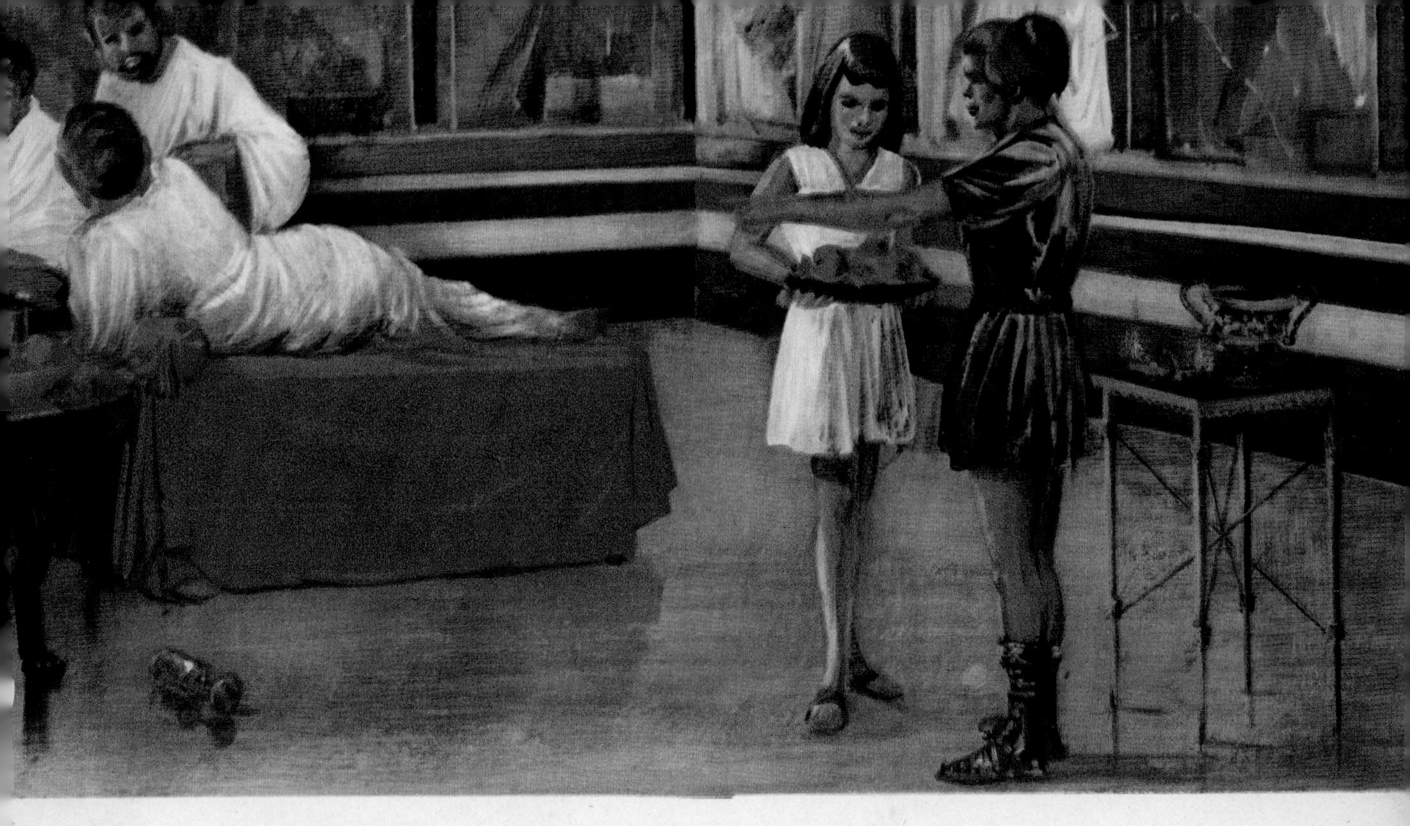

HOSTS VIED WITH EACH OTHER TO SERVE RARE DELICACIES.

pressive dinner had to have dozens of such dishes —whole fish cooked in a sea of shrimp, meats with spiced vegetables, meats with sauces, oysters with sauces, broiled blackbirds and wood pigeons, Spanish wildfowl stuffed with Indian rice, berries still sparkling with the morning's dew, peaches from Persia, and Greek wine to fill the golden goblets.

"We rise from table pale with overeating," the poet Horace wrote when he came home from one such dinner. He also said that the tablecloths were dirty.

Horace knew his way around Rome. His father had been a slave who earned his freedom, made a fortune, and bought his son the best Roman-Greek education. By the time Horace grew up, he had seen every side of the city and it had few surprises for him. But wherever he went, he found something that amused or annoyed him. There was a young man tugging nervously at his very fancy, very new toga; and the banker's wife, who wore too much jewelry and too short a skirt. There was the man who put on the airs of a gentleman and stole a chicken leg from the plate of the man who sat next to him at dinner. Horace put them all into poems, with a good dose of laughter and common sense. Comic luxury and dreadful poverty rubbed shoulders in the streets of Augustus' city, and the gay life of the rich was very different from the misery of the poor in the crowded slums. Horace could not call all of it good, but it was all a part of the adventure of Rome. In his poems, called *Satires, Epistles* and *Odes,* he poked fun at the Romans, and lectured them too. The lectures won him the favor of Augustus, who asked him to be his private secretary. Horace refused. It would have taken up most of his time, and it would have confined him to the city.

Sometimes the city was too much even for Horace, and then he would flee to his cottage in the country. Not the Princeps himself could persuade him to give up his peaceful vacations, during which he could relax on his quiet hill and shock his friend Virgil with the latest tale of the scandalous doings in Rome.

VIRGIL'S EPIC POEM

For Virgil, who was also a poet, the city was no adventure; it was a horror. He said that the good Rome and the good Romans—the kind of men who had won the world—could only be found now in the smaller towns and countryside of Italy. When Virgil wrote poetry, it was about the open fields and the clean air he loved. His first long poem, the *Georgics,* told of the joys of planting and harvesting, and of the men who were Rome's strength. When Augustus heard him read the poem, he was delighted, for this was the Italy he loved, too. Like Virgil, he had been raised in a little country town. And he, too, believed that Rome's hope was in the land and in a return to the old ways, which the city people had forgotten.

Virgil decided to write a book for Augustus. He would tell the story of the founding of Rome, in an epic poem, like the ones that Homer had written. It would honor Augustus and show all the world that his nation, like Homer's Greece, was a land of heroes. Virgil began with the story of Aeneas, who, he said, was the ancestor of Caesar and Augustus. For eleven years he worked to make his poem as great as Rome itself, but he was never satisfied with it. When he was dying, he ordered his friends to burn it. It was not good enough, he said, not good enough for Augustus and Rome. But Augustus commanded Virgil's friends to send the book to him. Soon all Rome had read it, and later it would be read by all the world. The *Aeneid,* as Virgil named it, became as famous as the *Iliad* and the *Odyssey,* and Virgil was called the Homer of Rome.

THE LUXURIOUS LIFE

Augustus had his own reasons for saving Virgil's poem. He hoped it would remind his people that courage, and not easy living, had won them their riches. It worried him that they could forget so much so easily. He was delighted when his historian, Livy, tried to stir up the old patriotism by writing the true stories of Rome's triumphs, from Romulus to Augustus in 142 volumes.

The Romans loved the *Aeneid* and they read Livy's history, or at least some of it. But they did not give up their comforts. Old Cato had been right—the riches of conquest were conquering Rome. Augustus was horrified to see that parents no longer taught their children Roman discipline. They laughed at traditions, forgot their ancestors, and ignored the gods. For many people, the idea of the family and its *pater familias* had become a joke. Elegant ladies collected husbands as eagerly as rich men collected statues. They turned love into a contest, a game they played just to keep busy.

Catullus, a young man who came to Rome in Caesar's time, had not understood the rules of this game. He loved only once. When he met Clodia, one of the grandest ladies in the city, he knew that she was the most beautiful woman he had ever seen. He was young and of no importance; she was ten years older than he, and the most famous people in Rome were her friends. But Catullus dared to send her a poem. It was a cautious little poem about a bird she kept in her house. When Clodia read it, she did not become angry. Instead, she asked him to write more poems for her. Then, because they were good poems and Catullus was as handsome as he was young, she fell in love with him. But after a time, she fell in love with someone else. Catullus could not change his love that easily, and he could not forget her. He wrote more poems—bitter, sad, and still full of love. Only Sappho in ancient Greece had written such love poetry before.

But by Augustus' time, the young men who came to the city had learned the rules of the game very well. They had money, and little to do with their time. That gave them the chance to follow what the Greek philosophers called their "individual pursuits." For young men—and some who were not so young—that usually meant the pursuit of women. When they needed advice, they turned to the verses of Ovid, a poet who wrote of love in a quite different way.

Ovid's book, *The Art of Love,* was a set of instructions in romance, elegantly phrased but very clear. Chapter One told "How to Find Her"; Chapter Two, "How to Win Her"; Chapter Three, "How to Keep Her." For women, there was a special section, "How to Win Him." A little later, Ovid published a second volume, "How to Get Rid of Her (or Him)." The books set all of Rome chuckling and winking until Augustus banished the poet for having written them.

Ovid was shipped off to a little town on the Black Sea. It was lonely there, and very far from Rome. He wrote no more about love, but he finished a great book of stories, the *Metamorphoses.* In it he retold the old myths, such as those of Narcissus, who sat so long admiring his own reflection in a pool that the gods turned him into a flower, and of King Midas, whose touch turned everything to gold.

Ovid was not the only light-hearted Roman who

found himself in trouble with the Princeps. Augustus banished his own granddaughter for her scandalous behavior. He wrote new laws to limit spending and wild behavior in the city. One of his laws even limited the quantity of wine a man could drink with his dinner. But such laws did little good. The Romans did not learn to behave or save their money; they simply learned not to get caught. And Augustus, who could usually find a solution for any problem, failed to turn his giddy citizens into the sober, old-fashioned Romans he wanted them to be.

THE FATHER OF HIS COUNTRY

Changing the world was a much easier job. The problems of the empire were practical ones, and Augustus tackled them with the same good sense that helped him straighten out the politics of Rome. He cleared the roads of robbers and chased the pirates off the sea routes. One by one, he took charge of the provinces himself. No one objected, because the governors he appointed took their posts to govern, not to loot. They were the beginning of a civil service, a corps of men whose lives were spent managing the affairs of government.

Above all else, Augustus kept the peace. Farmers could plant their fields, certain that the crops would not be trampled or burned by armies fighting civil wars. The streets of Italian cities no longer echoed with the frightening sounds of marching feet and harsh commands. Augustus gradually pulled his legions out of the peninsula, and then out of the provinces. He sent them to the frontiers, to guard against the barbarians and jealous eastern kings who threatened the new peace of the empire.

Augustus himself went to inspect the defenses and to visit the cities that now called him their only ruler. He returned with an idea for one more project—an Altar of Peace. He chose to put it on the Campus Martius, the field that from ancient times had belonged to the god of war. On the sides of the temple in which the altar would stand, he had his sculptors carve figures of Aeneas, Romulus and Remus, the Goddess Roma, and the goddess Earth. Then, around the top of the building, binding Earth and Rome and its founders together, he had them carve a procession of triumph. It showed Augustus leading the people as they took their offerings of thanks to the gods who had given them peace.

There were many people in the empire who thanked Augustus as well as the gods. On one of his journeys, when his royal yacht passed an Alexandrian merchant ship, he saw that the passengers and crew were lined up at the rail. They were dressed all in white and wore garlands, as if for some ceremony. Then he heard their voices across the water. They were indeed performing a ceremony. It was meant to honor him, and they were calling out their thanks for the good life, the wealth, and the freedom to sail the seas which he had brought them.

Order and peace were the gifts Augustus gave to Rome in return for his power. When he had established them and built a government to protect them, they lasted for nearly two hundred years. Toward the end of his reign, Augustus sat down to write a history of his years as Rome's ruler. Caesar would have been puzzled by it, for it was so short that it could all be engraved on two bronze tablets. In one of the last paragraphs, Augustus wrote: "While I was administering my thirteenth consulship, the senate and the knights and all the people gave me the title 'Father of my Country.' " He was prouder of this title, the gift of his citizens, than of any he had won by victory in war or power in politics.

In A.D. 14, Augustus died. For nearly forty-five years he had been the *pater familias* of Rome. In every city of the Roman world, men and women went to their temples to pray. They prayed to many different gods—in Rome, to Jupiter; in Athens, to Zeus; in Alexandria, to Isis and Ra. But they all made the same prayer: "Send us another Augustus so that we can live in peace."

WITH ITALY AT PEACE, AUGUSTUS SENT HIS LEGIONS TO THE EMPIRE'S FRONTIERS.

The Emperors' City

A.D. 14-A.D. 117

GREAT power had allowed Augustus to do great good for Rome and its provinces. The same power in the hands of a man who was not good meant that he could do great harm. This the Romans learned as they watched the remarkable parade of good and evil men who came to govern Rome after Augustus. Some of them were wise, two or three were foolish, one thought he was the greatest artist in the world, and another said he was a god. But all were the masters of Rome, mighty princes who were called emperors. The title emperor came from *imperator,* the Roman name for the man who commanded the armies. Every ruler of the empire owed his power to the legions. When he gave an order, his soldiers made certain that it was obeyed. And, if his orders became too harsh to bear, it was his soldiers who struck him down.

Augustus, like Caesar, had named the commander who would take his place when he died. The man he chose was one of his own family, the Caesars. So were the next three emperors. Two of these emperor Caesars were good and two were dreadfully bad.

The first, Augustus' stepson Tiberius, was good, though the city mob did not think so. He treated them with scorn, and, worse, he was stingy with his gifts of food and gave them very few shows. The Senate liked him even less than the people did. Tiberius was proud and he made it difficult for them to pretend that they were ruling Rome. Then, one morning, someone overheard him exclaim, as he was leaving the Senate house, "These senators, how ready they are to be slaves!" The senators, who remembered Caesar as well as Augustus, began to plot against the emperor. But he brought his own bodyguard to Rome—a hand-picked corps of legionaries called the Praetorian Guard. The Senate stopped plotting and waited hopefully for Tiberius to die.

THE MAD EMPEROR

In the provinces, however, the emperor was loved. If he was stern, he was also fair. When an official suggested rough methods for squeezing more tax money from the empire, Tiberius told him sharply, "A good shepherd shears his sheep, he does not beat them." To men who had suf-

COINS CARRIED REMINDERS OF THE EMPERORS' DEEDS THROUGH ALL THE EMPIRE.

fered under the old governors, that seemed like kindness.

Everything about Tiberius began to seem kindly when he was dead and Augustus' great-grandson Caligula became emperor. People suspected that he had murdered Tiberius. Some said that he had poisoned him, others that Tiberius was already sick and Caligula simply set a pillow over his face to hurry things along. Nevertheless, Caligula gave a solemn funeral speech for Tiberius and wept all the way through it.

Perhaps they were tears of joy, for Caligula loved being the emperor. As a boy, he had played soldier, dressed in a little legionary's uniform and boots. As emperor, he could play at being a god. He built a temple to himself, and a special bridge from his palace to the temple of Jupiter so that he could visit his "brother god." Then he collected Greek statues of gods, had the heads sawed off, and carvings of his own head placed on them.

Before long, hundreds of Romans were suffering the same fate as the statues, but without the benefit of new heads. Having emptied the state treasury, Caligula began to use Sulla's old system for raising money—kill the rich and take their property. Then he had people murdered for no reason at all. When he began to call Rome "the city of necks waiting for me to chop them," the Romans realized with horror that he was not just cruel, but mad.

The Praetorians, the royal guard, took care of the problem. One of their officers went to the arena where Caligula was attending the games. He waited in a hallway under the grandstand. When Caligula came out of the arena, the officer struck him with his dagger. The emperor fell, and his cries were drowned out by the shouts of the crowd above, cheering the gladiators. The guardsmen then rushed to the palace to capture Caligula's courtiers. They found his uncle, Claudius, shivering in fear behind a curtain, and dragged him out. Instead of killing him, they made him the emperor. It was the first time that soldiers had chosen a ruler for Rome. It would not be the last.

After Claudius got over his surprise, he began to act like an emperor. It was not easy for him. He was elderly and sensible, not at all like his wild young nephew Caligula, but no one had ever paid much attention to him before. Now everyone turned to him, and he was not always sure about what to do. Wisely, he followed Augustus' plans for running the empire. To help him carry them out, he chose a council of learned Greeks. They served him and the empire well. He also chose four wives, who served him badly. Each was worse than the one before. While the world trembled at Claudius' words, at home in the palace he was henpecked.

His last wife, Agrippina, was a battleship among women, who wheedled and nagged him. She had married him, it was said, only because she could not be emperor herself. He did not have to bear her sharp tongue for long, however. When she had persuaded him to name her own son Nero as his heir, she fed him some poisoned mushrooms, and Claudius ceased to be emperor as suddenly as he had begun.

ART AND MURDER

Nero, the new emperor, was just sixteen. With his mother to guide him and an empire to spoil him, he grew up to be the worst ruler in the history of Rome. He started off well enough. He ignored Agrippina and chose two able, honest men to advise him. His old tutor, the philosopher Seneca, took charge of the government and its officials. Burrus, the commander of the Praetorian Guard, looked after the armies. The young emperor spent his time on things that he felt were more important—singing, acting, painting pictures, writing poetry, and playing the lyre, the organ, and the bagpipe.

Nero was sure he was a great artist. And if he was not, no man in Rome dared say so. In the Senate, however, the graybeards shook their heads and worried about the future of the empire. They were horrified when Nero acted in the public theater. Actors were not respectable citizens, they said. Neither were singers and dancers, but Nero invited them all to the palace.

The people loved it. An emperor out to have fun was something new. Of course, the old Greek tragedies he staged for them were dull, but when they booed, he brought back the wild animals and the gladiators. There was more free food, too. The Senate might complain, but Nero spent his money freely. And the scandals of his court, where lords acted like street musicians and street musicians acted like lords and ladies, brought the mob some new excitement every day.

Meanwhile, Agrippina fumed. It was not so much the scandal that bothered her. But she had no chance to take a hand in the ruling of the empire. She lectured Nero, calling his advisers scoundrels, thieves, and worse. She coaxed him. She threatened to make his stepbrother the emperor in his place. When she had had her say and Nero was feeling grumpy, Seneca and Burrus dug into the treasury and gave him money enough to put on a new spectacle. They applauded his latest poem, bought him a Greek chariot to drive around the Circus Maximus, and then got back to their work of governing the empire. And Nero, cheerful again, had his stepbrother murdered.

Things went on this way for several years, with the emperor's mother scolding him and his advisers comforting him at the treasury's expense. Then Agrippina made the mistake of telling Nero not to marry a girl he had fallen in love with. Nero decided it was time for his mother to join Claudius in the underworld. Agrippina, however, was very wise in the ways of royal murder, and she did not take chances. Three times Nero fed her poison; each time she had taken the antidote first. He had his workmen build a machine that would drop the bedroom ceiling on her, but she was warned about it. He sent her for a cruise on a ship specially designed to fall apart at sea, but she was a strong swimmer. Finally, he sent the army, and Agrippina never lectured him again.

Burrus and Seneca left him, too—Burrus died and Seneca retired. Without their help, Nero was soon in trouble and the empire was in debt. When he began to use Sulla's kill-the-rich system, the senators began to plot against him. Then disaster struck Rome, and, suddenly, everything else was forgotten.

THE BURNING OF ROME

On the night of July 18, in A.D. 64, a fire broke out in the wooden bleachers of the Circus Maximus. Within minutes, all of the tinder-dry stadium was ablaze. A wind carried the sparks to the houses nearby, and they, too, burst into flames. The fire raced through the cheaply-built tenements along the narrow old streets, jumped to the wooden roofs of temples and baths, and roared along the colonnades crowded with shops. Nothing could stop it. Merchants and soldiers, rich men and slaves—anyone who lived near the fire ran to the fields outside the city. As the flames spread to other sections of the city, the roads became jammed with carts and wagons loaded down with the furniture, statues, gold plates, and finery that people hoped to save. Nero himself left for his villa in the country. For six days, the fire burned. When the Romans dared to come back to the city, ten of its fourteen districts were in ashes.

Nero returned, and, for once, went to work eagerly. He called for his architects and designed a new Rome, with straight wide streets and buildings of stone and brick instead of wood. For his own use he planned a fantastic palace that was a city in itself. Its pillared arcade was a mile long. It had a vast lake surrounded with buildings made to look like little towns. The emperor's garden included fields and vineyards and a forest with wild animals. Some of the rooms in the palace itself had painted walls, but Nero's own apartments were plated with gold and decorated with jewels. The ceilings were designed to slide back so that showers of flowers or perfume could be sprinkled on the people below. The "Golden House" of Rome soon was known all over the world, and, to remind everyone who had built it, at the entrance stood a statue of Nero, twelve stories high.

The emperor had such a good time building his new Rome that someone suggested that he had set the fire himself. Every gossip in the city had already told and retold the story about his reciting poetry to the music of a lyre while the city burned. The new rumor was just as easy to believe.

Nero had not started the fire. But, as the stories

FLOWERS WERE SCATTERED THROUGH THE SLIDING CEILINGS OF THE GOLDEN HOUSE.

spread, he had to find someone to take the blame. He chose the Christians. They were a new religious group and troublesome, because they refused to worship the emperor. Their first leader—the reports in Rome called him Christus—had been put to death by a Roman governor during the reign of Tiberius. But his followers had gone on preaching his un-Roman ideas, and these followers seemed to get more numerous all the time. Nero had the Christians in the city rounded up. Then he invited all of Rome to come into the garden of his new palace to watch while some of the prisoners, dressed in animal skins, were attacked by ferocious hunting dogs. The rest of the Christians were killed off in a show at the Circus. Nero took charge of the performance himself, standing in a chariot and dressed as a Greek charioteer.

But the Romans were not pleased with the games. "Who knows if these Christians set the fire?" they asked. "What good can their deaths do Rome now?" And they told each other that the emperor enjoyed his killings too much. They had seen his brutality before; one day it might touch them.

But the emperor was busy with plans for games of a less painful sort. He had decided to give the Greeks an opportunity to see his skill in their arts. He went on a tour of Greece, and commanded that the Olympics and other great contests be held while he was there. Then he entered every singing, harp-playing, and chariot-racing competition at all of them. He won every time. This was not surprising, for it was dangerous to out-do the emperor. The cheering was less loud than he had hoped for, but he came back to Rome with 1,080 first prizes.

Meanwhile, the city buzzed with plots against him. Many of the great men in Rome were involved in them, despite the danger. Seneca, who had been the emperor's adviser, joined one of the groups of plotters and was killed when Nero discovered it. The execution angered Rome and more of Nero's friends learned to hate him. Anger grew in the provinces, too, and the legions began to turn against the emperor. When the news reached the capital, the Senate found its courage. It voted to condemn Nero as an enemy of Rome, and the Praetorians, his own guard, refused to protect him.

Defenseless, knowing that he was about to be arrested, Nero fled his Golden House and ran to the home of one of the few friends he had left. When the soldiers knocked at the door, he stabbed himself. "I go and the world loses a great artist!" he moaned. Then he died, and so, in A.D. 68, the line of the Caesars came to an end.

Now there was no one who had a true claim to the throne of Augustus. However, the Praetorian Guard had made Claudius an emperor, and they were willing to try again. When they announced their choice, three of the legions, not wanting to be left out, named candidates of their own. For a year the empire had too many emperors and no order at all.

AFTER THE FALL OF JERUSALEM, TITUS CARRIED THE TEMPLE ORNAMENTS IN HIS GREAT TRIUMPH.

Finally one general, Flavian Vespasianus, who had the troops of the eastern frontier to argue his rights for him, claimed the throne. The Senate agreed to let him keep it, and for twelve years he and his sons ruled Rome. The Golden House was torn down, for Vespasian preferred to live in Augustus' house on the Palatine Hill. Gilded walls and playing the artist were not for him. In fact, three years before he became the emperor, his army career—and his life—had nearly come to a sudden end when he fell asleep at one of Nero's song recitals. Now that Rome was his, he intended to bring order, not music, to the empire.

His methods were not always gentle ones. When the Jews of Jerusalem revolted against the emperor whom they, like the Christians, would not call a god, Vespasian sent his son Titus to destroy them. After a siege that lasted for six months, Titus captured the city and slaughtered more than a million Jews.

Strangely enough, this same Titus, who became emperor when his father died, was called in Rome "the delight of mankind." He became famous for his kindness, though perhaps the Romans were only impressed with the enormous stadium which he and his father built for them. It was called the Colosseum. Forty to fifty thousand people could watch the gladiators from the marble seats in its grandstands, protected from the sun by huge awnings manned by sailors of the imperial fleet. The outside of the stadium was just as grand—four tiers of columns and arches, set one upon another. It was a gift to win any emperor a name for generosity.

But Titus' reign was remembered as much for nature's cruelty as the emperor's kindness. In the short two years that he ruled Rome, one disaster after another came to Italy. There was an outbreak of the plague, then another fire in the city. In A.D. 79, the volcano Vesuvius suddenly erupted, raining fire and molten lava on the busy town of Pompeii. When the volcano grew calm again and the smoke drifted away, Pompeii had disappeared. The town, its buildings, and its people lay buried under a blanket of ashes in a tomb of lava rock.

However, the rest of the Roman world was soon back to normal. The plague died down, Rome was built up again, and there was a new emperor without an ounce of kindness in him. He was Titus' brother Domitian, and he set out to keep the peace no matter what cruelty was necessary to do it. His harshness shocked and frightened Rome. And, when people began to speak out against him, his own fear and suspicion drove him to even greater cruelty. It became dangerous to talk in the streets, because the emperor imagined plots where there were none. Of course, when he punished people for imaginary plots, the real plotting began. Finally, his rages made even his friends afraid for their lives, and he was murdered by his officers and his wife.

"PEACE, NOT WAR"

Rome had had enough of military rulers. When Domitian was out of the way. the Senate was quick to name its own man as the emperor, before the legions had a chance to act. But the man they had chosen, Nerva, lived for only two years. That was just time enough for him to learn that it took a soldier, not a senator, to control the armies which gave the emperor his power. With the Senate's approval, Nerva adopted as his heir a general from Spain. His name was Trajan, and he rivalled Caesar in his ability to command troops.

Trajan dreamed of adding new lands to the empire. For five years, from A.D. 101 to 106, he and his soldiers battled the Dacians, the fierce barbarians who held the territory beyond the Danube. The legions were in top fighting form and their emperor was the finest commander under whom they had ever served. When he returned to Italy, Dacia was a province of Rome. Trajan celebrated his victories by building a huge new forum in the city. In its center, he set up a stone column with carvings that told the whole story of the war.

A few years later, Trajan marched the legions against the Asians in the Tigris-Euphrates valley. But his new campaign was not a success, and finally he had to admit that it was senseless to go on with it. Worn out and disappointed, he began the journey back to Rome. On the way, he was taken ill and died.

Hadrian, the new emperor, was as brilliant a soldier as Trajan. But like Augustus, he was also a statesman. He knew that the Roman world had needs that were more important than extra land. It needed his legions to keep its frontiers safe, and his treasury and his laws to make life better on the land it already owned. "The business of the emperor," Hadrian said, "is peace, not war."

Rome's days of conquest were over.

THE EMPEROR HADRIAN

The City of the World

A.D. 117-A.D. 138

ROME was no longer just a city—it was a world. In the reign of Hadrian, the blaring trumpets that announced the comings and goings of the emperor echoed in Spain and Syria and Britain as often as in Italy. Hadrian wanted to know what was going on in all of his empire. He wanted to inspect the troops and forts that held the frontiers, and to judge for himself the wisdom of the governors he had sent to rule the provinces. He wanted to visit the towns and cities, to see their ancient buildings, to plan new buildings where they were needed, and to build new towns in the frontier provinces. And he wanted to meet the people. They were citizens of Rome, even though their homes were hundreds of miles from Italy and they had never seen the Forum. Hadrian's journey through the empire took eight years. He followed the Roman roads and the sea routes Rome had freed from pirates, until he had visited every part of the world of which he was the sole, all-powerful ruler.

He met many other travelers on the roads. Travel was easy now, and safe. Rich Romans, imitating the emperor, had become eager tourists. They flocked to Greece; to them it was a quaint place out of another age. They studied its famous buildings, bought statues and pottery for souvenirs, and paced out the old battlefields which they had read about in Plutarch's histories. In Egypt, they went shopping in Alexandria, still handsome and a bustling center of trade. They rode in elegant comfort on sightseeing barges that took them up the Nile to Memphis and Thebes. There they admired the oldest buildings known to man, and scratched their initials in the stonework.

This eastern area was Rome's "Old World." It had charming but outdated Greek towns and bustling Alexandrian cities, where everyone spoke Greek. In the west, however, there was a modern land, a world that Rome had built. In Gaul and the German lands, in North Africa, in Spain and Britain, Hadrian looked with pride at new cities standing on the old barbaric hills. They were as fine as any cities in the east.

At Athens, Hadrian had gone to see for himself the buildings called the most beautiful in the world, and he had agreed that they were splendid. Then he had come upon the foundations and a few lonely columns of the gigantic temple which an Athenian tyrant, Pisistratus, had begun six hundred years before. It was a project so impossibly big that no other ruler of Athens had tried to finish it. Hadrian looked it over, called for his own workmen, and the temple was completed. It had taken a Greek to imagine it, but a Roman to build it.

That was the story in all of the empire. Romans looked for the jobs that needed doing and got them done. Unlike the Greeks, their scientists did not ask "Why?" They asked: "How?"—"How does it work?"—"How does it fit together?"—"How can we use it?" The Romans borrowed the Greek builders' designs just as they borrowed the Greek teachers' ideas, because they were good and they worked. It was constructing buildings, not designing them, that excited a Roman builder. His art was engineering.

No project was impossible for Roman engineers, and the bigger, the better. They constructed theaters that could hold 80,000 people. They built mile after mile of fine roads across deserts and mountains to the edges of the Roman world. Their bridges and aqueducts spanned rivers and gorges with arches of stone. The Etruscans had taught the first Romans the trick of building an archway of wedge-shaped stones fitted together so that they could not fall. In the seven or eight hundred years since then, their pupils had become master builders who used the arches to give strength to some of the biggest structures man had ever made. In Hadrian's homeland, Spain, they had bridged the great Tagus Gorge. The largest of the bridge's six arches was 90 feet wide and 150 feet tall. It was made of granite blocks, without mortar or braces to hold them in place. The two-storied aqueduct of Segovia, a stone canal to carry water from the mountains to the city, rested on 128 arches of uncemented stone. Two thousand years after it was built, the aqueduct was still being used. When the Romans discovered how to make concrete, there was no limit to what they could build. They set wide domes on their temples, instead of the old wooden roofs. In every corner of the empire, they built arches that were wider, taller, and stronger than before. For centuries the arches would stand, a sign that the Romans had come that way.

HADRIAN'S TRAVELS

The new cities had that Roman stamp, too. Each was a little Rome, with its Forum, senate house, theater, library, and well-paved streets. Men whose barbarian fathers had lived in huts and fought in the wilderness, now lived in Roman houses, worshiped Roman gods in Roman temples, and cheered the charioteers in Roman arenas.

Hadrian was more than a royal tourist in these western cities, and he was no foreign overlord. He spoke to the people in the Latin they spoke. He shared their worries about trade or the crops. And, wherever he went, people knew his face, because they saw it every time they went shopping or counted their money. Roman coins were marked with a portrait of the emperor. It was a handy way to put a reminder of him in every home in the empire. The inscriptions on the coins were carefully chosen to point out to the people the good things that this emperor was doing for them. "Hadrian, the generous giver of money to the poor," they said, or, "Hadrian who built the temple of Roma and Venus." Several times a year, the words were changed, so that the latest news of the emperor's good works could be sent hurrying from hand to hand across the Roman world. When he traveled, new coins were issued announcing his arrival in the various provinces. For peaceful provinces, the inscriptions read, "Hadrian, the bringer of order and wealth." For places where there was unrest or rebellion, the words were, "Hadrian, commander of great and powerful armies." And, year after year, there were coins that carried the emperor's favorite message, "Hadrian, like Augustus, the father of his country."

When Hadrian spoke to the people, he called them citizens, and most of them now were. They shared the protection of his legions and the justice of Roman law. No angry governor could sentence them to torture or to death, for they had the right to "appeal to Caesar," which meant a trial in Rome. Under Hadrian, the harsh laws of the old Rome—the city—had been changed to deal fairly with the people of the new Roman world.

From Antioch to London, Hadrian was the first citizen of that huge Rome. He was the leader of sixty-five to one hundred million people who were held together by their loyalty to one government, Hadrian's government. In Hadriana, a town he founded in the East, a philosopher-poet wrote a song of praise about the city that became an empire: "To Rome's rule we owe it that the wide world is our home, that we are all one people, citizens of Rome." The Greek philosophers had imagined such a world, where all mankind was one. Alexander the Great had dreamed of shaping such a world by conquest. But, again, it had taken a Roman to build it.

And it took strong Roman walls to guard it. The Atlantic Ocean and the deserts of the Sahara protected Rome on two sides, but along the other frontiers there were barbarians and Asian kings. Ceaselessly they beat against the defenses, always hoping to find a weak place, to break through, and to rob and plunder the rich lands on the other side. When Hadrian came to Britain, he

HADRIAN'S VILLA AT TIVOLI REFLECTED THE CALMNESS OF HIS EMPIRE.

saw the ravages made by savage Picts and Celts, who had made raids from Scotland. He ordered his soldiers to build a wall, a wall of concrete faced with stone, twenty feet high and eight feet thick, across the entire width of Britain. Hadrian himself paced out the line of the wall and planned the castles for the soldiers who would guard it. Then his troops built it, just as they built a wall of upright oak logs, nine feet high, that ran the 345 miles between the Rhine and Danube rivers on the German frontier.

Where there were no walls of stone or logs, there were walls of men. Rome's legions numbered hundreds of thousands. Italians, Britons, Africans, Spaniards, Egyptians, and Gauls fought side by side. They guarded the Roman world's most treasured possession—the *Pax Romana,* the Peace of Rome. It gave order to the empire, brought wealth to its people, and kept war outside its borders.

Rome had taken on an enormous and difficult job—to make a Roman city of the world, to put a wall around it, and to rule it well. When Hadrian came home from his long journey, he thought that perhaps it could be done. The Romans had always taken on big jobs. They were men of action. They had been that way even years ago when, as the people of a little country town, they had tried to conquer all of Italy. Virgil had recognized this when he wrote his great poem for Augustus and expressed what it meant to be a Roman:

Other men, I know, will shape fine bronze
Into statues that seem to breathe, and carve from marble
Faces as real as life. Others will speak
With finer words than ours, or learn to chart
The map of the sky, the circling journeys of the planets
And where the stars will rise. But Roman, remember:
To rule the nations wisely with fair laws,
To bring them peace forever, to destroy the warlike
And treat the conquered kindly. These are our arts.

The City Where Money Ruled

A.D. 54-A.D. 192

"IT IS impossible to find peace and quiet in this city!" Seneca, in Nero's Rome for a visit, was not enjoying his stay, and he wrote about it in an angry letter to one of his friends in the country. "The room I have rented is right over a public bath, and I might as well have taken a bed in the Tower of Babel. When the athletic bathers do their exercises, I hear every grunt as they strain to lift the dumbbells and the awful wheezes as they drop them again. In the ball court, a loud-mouthed coach calls out the score at the top of his voice. Then a rowdy starts a quarrel, a pickpocket gets caught in the act (he howls, of course), and some idiot chooses his bathtub as the place to sing a concert. There is a regular parade of human elephants flopping into the swimming pool, each trying to make a greater splash than the last, and a chorus of drink sellers, sausage vendors, pastrymen, and hawkers for the restaurants—each of them with his own noisy way of spoiling my rest and interrupting my work."

A bathhouse, with its pools and game rooms and restaurants and locker rooms, was probably as noisy as any spot in Rome. But Seneca would not have found much quiet in any neighborhood in the city. There were just too many people. In the years since Augustus had made Rome the capital of his empire, the city had grown bigger, busier, and noisier than ever. In the mornings, when the shops were open and the merchants' carts went out to make deliveries, it was hard to get through the streets at all. The tenements were jammed full. The great town houses overflowed with guests and slaves. And still the people poured into Rome. The citizens knew that the

IMPERIAL ROME WAS A CITY OF MONUMENTAL PUBLIC BUILDINGS.

empire was big and filled with thriving towns, but when they peered out of their windows, it looked as though everyone in the empire had decided to live in the capital.

"QUEEN MONEY"

The newcomers were here to make their fortunes. They had heard fantastic tales of the money that could be made in Rome, and some of the stories were true. Freed slaves and unknown merchants from foreign villages had set up shop in the city and had indeed become millionaires. They had moved into splendid houses and were treated as friends by men whose families had been famous in Rome for hundreds of years. They were introduced to the emperor, who made them welcome at the court, and they were given important government jobs. No one cared what they had been before. If they were rich, they were good Romans.

"In Rome, everything is the slave of Queen Money," Horace once wrote. "When a man has piled up enough gold, the world is eager to call him famous, courageous, and honest as well as rich.—And wise, too?—Wise, too, of course. Or king, if he likes, so long as he has the money."

In fact, no Roman millionaire quite managed to buy himself a kingdom from the emperor. But he could live like a king, and there were plenty of people who would tell him he was brave or wise if it meant that a little money would trickle out of his hand into theirs.

Rome and the Romans were very different from what they once had been. Horace said the city had gone mad—money-mad. But the race to get rich was only one sign of the change. In the old days, when the city was always at war, the citizens had had no time for anything except fighting to win new land or to keep the land they already owned. All their gold went to pay for ships and soldiers. There were jobs to be done, and everyone pitched in. Then came the emperors and the peace that won the Romans the praise of the people they had conquered. In Rome itself, the citizens had money in their pockets and plenty of leisure time. They went on a mammoth spending spree, rushing to enjoy themselves as they never had before. Later, when there were fewer and fewer jobs to be done, passing the time became a job in itself. Rich men gave their gold to find new ways to keep busy. The mob shouted for more shows in the arenas. Queen Money paid the bills, and "More and Bigger" was everybody's slogan.

Once Cicero had asked if a man could really find pleasure in watching another man being mangled by a huge animal, or a jungle beast being tortured until it died. Now, tens of thousands of Romans, who crowded into the stadiums a hundred or more times a year, would have answered, "Yes!" They wanted naval battles, too, like the one Augustus gave for them, and giraffes and elephants as well as lions. They turned the old Greek plays into Roman spectacles. Cicero saw a performance of a tragedy that had 600 mules in the cast. When Horace went to the theater, he complained that there were so many troops of horsemen, war chariots, carriages, and ships rattling across the stage that nobody noticed the play.

CULTURE AND CRUELTY

In early Rome, when the city was still struggling to hold its own against Carthage, the actors had played good Roman comedies. The citizens listened closely, at least to the jokes. For years, the Romans' favorite playwright, Plautus, kept them laughing with new plays that told old stories—about the *pater familias* who was henpecked by his wife and made foolish by his sons, or the bullying officer who bragged about his bravery and ran for his life when a slave boy shouted, "Boo!" The shows were noisy, the comedians made fun of people in the audience, and often their jokes were bad. Then Terence, a young dandy, began to write plays of a different kind. They pleased the young fellows who came home from college in Greece convinced that Rome and their fathers were shockingly old-fashioned and slow-witted. Terence borrowed his stories from the Greek comedies, and he filled them with clever speeches and puns that every young Roman tried to imitate. Enjoying his plays meant keeping both ears open. But, over the years, more scenery, animals and crowds, and fantastic costumes were added to the plays, until the audience grew more interested in what they could see than in what they could hear. Often they could not hear even if they wanted to. In Augustus' time, Horace said that the noise of beasts and machines on the stage was so loud that the actors could barely shout above it. Horace lost his temper altogether when a lady sitting next to him clapped for an actor before he had even begun to say his speech. His robe was such a pretty new shade of purple, she said.

Nero had added his own touches to the dramas. When the story called for a character to die, he had a prisoner dressed up in a costume, pushed onto the stage, and actually killed. Nero also tried to make the Roman theater more Greek. When the mob booed his tragedies because they were too dull, he did not give up. He had his tutor, Seneca, write fine Latin versions of the old tragic stories, which he and his friends acted privately in the palace. Seneca's plays were good; 1,500 years later, playwrights in Europe were still imitating them.

It was fortunate for the world that Nero enjoyed acting in plays more than writing them. If he had wanted to be a playwright, Seneca's tragedies might never have been performed at all. The emperor did not like competition, as Seneca's young nephew, Lucan, learned to his sorrow. Lucan wrote poetry, and so did Nero. But Lucan's poetry was better than the emperor's. When the Romans began to praise the poems Lucan read to them, Nero commanded him never to read them in public again. The young poet was so angry that he joined a plot against the emperor and lost his life.

A wiser poet than Lucan was Petronius, one of Nero's courtiers. He wrote the witty and wicked sort of verses for which Ovid had been sent into exile. Nero loved them, but Petronius never admitted that he had written them. For the stories, which he called *The Satyricon,* poked fun at the court and at the courtiers who often made fools of themselves. Petronius was an old friend of Nero's and knew that the emperor might laugh at a joke one day and take it seriously the next. As it happened, Petronius got into trouble despite his caution. Another man in the court, jealous of his friendship with Nero, began to spread the false rumor that he was mixed up in a plot. Petronius was condemned to death, not for the book he had written, but for a crime he had not done. It would have made another good story for *The Satyricon,* if he had lived to write it.

THE MASSIVE BATHS OF CARACALLA WERE A FAVORITE MEETING-PLACE FOR ROMANS.

There were many such stories in Rome, true stories of envy and murder, of cruelty, money-madness, poverty, and fear. In the years that followed Petronius' death, other writers painted a strange and frightening picture of the city. When Nero had been killed, the evils which should have died with him seemed to live on. While Trajan was fighting his great campaigns in the Danube territory, the poet Juvenal wandered about Rome, pushing his way through the crowds that were thicker than ever. And, on every side, he saw folly and evil. Rome was the nightmare city, Juvenal said. Wine that sparkled in a golden cup always held the threat of poison. Spies were everywhere; their gentle whispers meant that someone's throat would soon be cut. In all of the city, Juvenal could find no woman who was good, no man who was honest.

People said that Juvenal wrote with acid instead of ink—he spoke so sharply and never had a good word for Rome. Perhaps it was true that he had soured on life. Perhaps he saw the worst side of the city because that was what he looked for. But, Tacitus, a historian, seemed to agree with him. Tacitus set out to write the story of Rome and its emperors from Tiberius to Domitian, and he called it "a black and shameful age." Rome's great freedoms were gone, he said. They had been destroyed by ruthless rulers who forced honest men to keep their mouths and ears shut if they wanted to go on living. Tacitus had good reason to hate the emperors. He had lived through the harsh reign of Domitian, the emperor who punished men for plotting even before the plots had begun.

But there seemed to be another side of the story. Tacitus' friend, Pliny, saw nothing shameful in the Roman world. Pliny was one of Trajan's officials in the provinces. In the letters he wrote back to Rome, he talked about his work and the life he saw as hectic and busy, but not evil and certainly not unpleasant.

It was puzzling that the two friends could see the same things so differently—but, in fact, they did not see the same things. Tacitus, like Juvenal, spent most of his life in the city. Pliny went to the provinces, away from the court and the mob. The trouble was in the city of Rome itself.

When the emperor Hadrian journeyed through the empire, he saw rich land, prosperous towns, and people who seemed contented. But when he returned to Rome, he could feel that something here was wrong. It did not show on the face of the city, which was beautiful. Hadrian himself had added a dozen new buildings to the city, and had rebuilt the Pantheon so that it was more splendid than before. On every side, the wealth of Rome was displayed in fine houses, colonnades, shops, theaters, and temples. It was the richest city in the world, but far from the happiest. People spent money recklessly, only to find that it bought them little satisfaction. There was ugliness in Rome as well as beauty. And, though it was the most powerful city in the world, many of its citizens lived in fear.

The Romans had seen great cruelty—slaves beaten to death, criminals tortured and burned alive, and whole towns of Jews or Christians massacred. Such things were a part of everyday

RELIGIOUS CULTS, LIKE THAT OF ISIS, ATTRACTED MANY NEW FOLLOWERS IN ROME.

life, like the beatings which parents and schoolmasters gave to children who misbehaved or the killings that everyone cheered in the arenas. Indeed, many Romans thought that the gladiator shows were too tame. They called for fights without armor, so that the gladiators could kill each other sooner. After all, they said, the best part of the show was the moment when a victor stood over his beaten opponent, turned to the crowd, and at their thumbs-down signal drove his dagger into the other man's chest.

It was strange that the people who built their roads and bridges to last forever were so ready to destroy lives in a minute. But it was so, and Rome's slaves knew it as well as the gladiators did. According to the law, a man was not a man at all once he had been captured and shipped to Rome. He was a "tool that talked," something his master could use in any way he liked. Animals were "semi-talking tools," and hoes and ploughs were "silent tools." For many years, no law protected the slaves from even the cruelest masters. They were beaten with whips or with ropes into which bits of sharp stone had been woven. Runaways were branded. If a master lost his temper and killed a slave, no one interfered. Slaves were cheap; they cost less than good cattle. Some people said that an execution now and then was a good thing. It kept the other slaves in line. Of course, there were Romans who knew that their slaves were men like themselves, whatever the law said, and treated them kindly. After Spartacus' army of slaves had frightened all of Italy, laws were passed to control masters whose tempers were too sharp. Augustus, too, tried to make things easier for the slaves. He disapproved of killing as a punishment, and collars with name plates on them were used instead of branding. But a slave's life was still cheap, and thousands of them were worked to death.

FATE AND FORTUNE

The slave who won his freedom could never forget how little his life had once meant. No matter how rich or powerful he became, a little of the old fear still lived inside him. It was a feeling that his children and grandchildren knew, too, and in Hadrian's Rome almost ninety per cent of the people were freed slaves or the descendants of slaves.

Two new gods had come to Rome: Fate and Fortune. They were not the old-fashioned kind of gods with whom a man could strike a bargain. Fate had a plan for every person and every city; no one could change it. Fortune had no plan; she played with the lives of men, changing things as she pleased, for no reason. The people who believed in Fate and Fortune—and most Romans did—could do nothing except wait to see what these most powerful gods had in store for them. But they did not wait patiently. They had always watched for signs and omens, and now they tried in every way possible to find out what the future would bring.

THE MITHRA CULT SACRIFICED BULLS.

In the cellars and dark corners of the slums, poor men sought out the hags who were said to know black magic. Some were old country women, who mixed up harmless tonics and remedies from roots and herbs. Others called themselves witches. They brewed love potions and poisons, talked to ghosts, sold curses and charms to ward off curses, and foretold the future. For the rich, there were astrologers who read the future in the stars and went about their fortunetelling in an up-to-date, scientific way. The scientists at Alexandria had discovered that the movements of the moon had something to do with the rise and fall of ocean tides. After that, it was easy to believe that everything on earth, including the lives of men, was "moved" by the stars and planets. When certain stars shone in the sky, things went well, but others brought evil and bad luck. The astrologers claimed to know the powers of each star, and for a price they gave advice on the good or bad days for marrying, taking a journey, doing business, or planting crops. Sometimes they disagreed with each other, but that did not trouble their customers. Everyone was sure that his own stargazer was the one who knew the truth, and even the emperors trusted the wisdom of their favorite astrologers.

NEW GODS FOR ROME

Of course, it was not much good knowing the future if you could do nothing about it. When a man was told to expect the worst, he began to look desperately for hope. The old gods were no help to him. Jupiter and his family were too much like businessmen, and they did not seem to care about mankind. The gods of the East, however, were much more sympathetic. They could not make life easier by changing it, but they did promise to lead their followers to a new and better life in paradise after death. In the meantime, their feasts, sacrifices, and initiation ceremonies helped people to forget the pain or dullness which they could not avoid on earth.

With drums and cymbals, the priests of *Magna Mater,* the "Great Mother" of the universe, called her people to wild days of dancing and singing that turned into shrieks of fearful joy. The worshipers of Isis, the calm and beautiful goddess of Egypt, filed solemnly through the streets chanting hymns, or stood for hours in silence, gazing at the lovely, pitying face of her statue in a temple. Isis was the favorite god among the women. For the men, there was a more rugged Persian god, Mithra, the Lord of Light. He was also the god of strength and courage, and entire Roman legions dedicated themselves to him. In underground chapels, they celebrated Mithra's triumph over darkness and evil. The sacred ceremonies were performed by soldiers wearing the masks of the Raven, the Lion, the Sun-Runner, and the other characters in Mithra's story. As the torches burned brighter, the chants became shouts, the rites grew wilder, and it was said that sometimes they ended with the sacrifice of a man.

The other gods were usually satisfied with the blood of animals, but their celebrations were as frantic as Mithra's, especially in the springtime. They were gods who had conquered death, and every spring they proved their power by giving new life to nature. Their followers said it was a sign that they, too, would be given new lives when they died. When the first leaves appeared on the trees and plants began to poke through the earth, Rome became a city of festivals. The children of *Magna Mater* danced out of the city to a grove on a sacred hill, where they held a Feast of Joy that went on for twelve days and nights. On another hill, a noisier, rather giddy group of worshipers chanted praise for Bacchus, the god of wine and crops. He, too, had a story of death and rebirth, which gave his followers hope. So did his wine, which flowed among them as freely as the Tiber.

In the city, meanwhile, the Ship of Isis was drawn through the streets at the head of a gaudy procession of musicians and merrymakers in masks. The launching of the ship marked the start of a carnival. The revelers in their smiling masks danced and sang and forgot that the world could be hard. "I am what is, has been, and shall be," Isis had promised. It was a comfort to know that the past and future of mankind belonged to a goddess so loving and beautiful. "I conquer Fate and Fate obeys me," Isis said. And, like the joyful people on the hills, the men and women laughing in the streets of Rome knew that cruelty, hunger, and pain did not matter. Such things would only last for a little while, until death opened the door to a new and better life.

CHRISTIANS AND PHILOSOPHERS

The Christian god also offered the promise of life after death. He had many followers in Rome now, though they did not celebrate their festivals in the streets. The Christians usually met in secret. It was dangerous to attend their meetings, because they, like the Jews, refused to call the emperor a god. The people who worshiped Isis or Mithra or any of the other eastern gods did not have that problem. They could worship the emperor of Rome, too, and as many other gods as they liked. Often they paid their respects to several of the gods, just to be safe.

But there were some Romans who did not look

THE PARADE OF THE SHIP OF ISIS SIGNALED THE START OF A CARNIVAL, A TIME OF REVELRY FOR THE WORSHIPPERS OF THE EGYPTIAN GODDESS.

to the gods for safety or hope. Like the wise men of ancient Greece, they turned instead to philosophy to find the answers to their most troubling questions. Of course, Greek wisdom was not as easy to live with as Greek statues were. Philosophy asked much of a man, and gave back little that the world could see. It took discipline, too, and discipline was no longer a Roman practice.

Nero, who was eager to be Greek in everything, did manage to find a philosophy that fitted him quite comfortably. Epicurean philosophy, it was called. Nero said that it taught the lesson, "Eat, drink, and be merry, for tomorrow you die." And, when he was dead, no one could deny that he had proven the truth of the lesson. He had worked hard at enjoying himself, and his enemies had seen to the rest. Apparently his tutor, Seneca, had been afraid to tell him that he was completely wrong about Epicurean philosophy. It was supposed to teach people to enjoy things wisely, without overdoing anything. Or perhaps Seneca knew that, for Nero, philosophy, like poetry, would always mean what Nero said it meant.

Seneca himself had other ideas about philosophy. He was a Stoic, a follower of Zeno of Athens, and he believed that true wisdom gave a man the strength to meet his fate nobly, without flinching. Seneca's strong will helped him to become the most powerful adviser in the palace. He had the courage to give up his power and to plot against the emperor when he knew that it was for the good of Rome. And, when Nero condemned

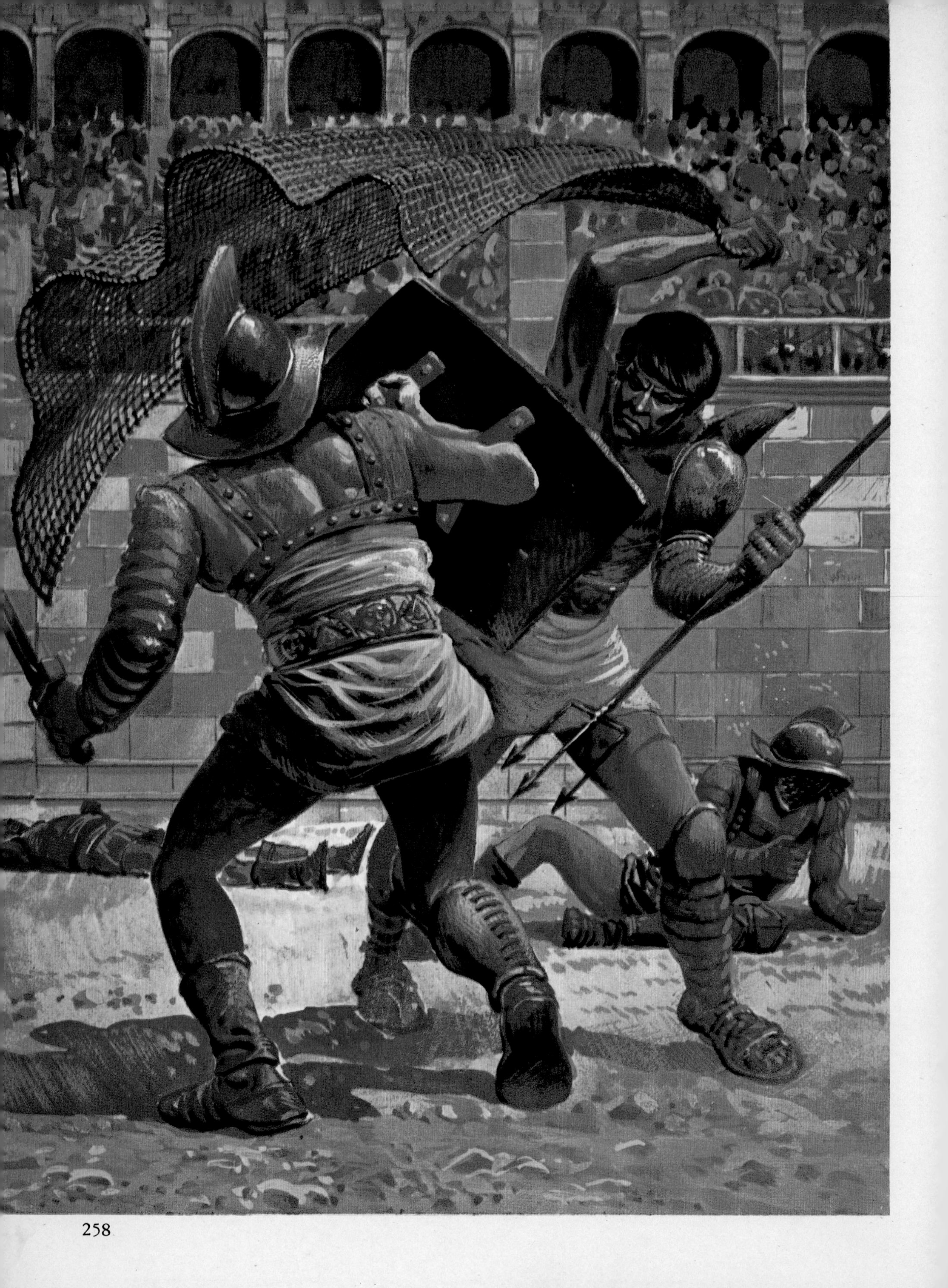

him to death, he did not wait for the executioner. He said good-by to his friends, finished the work he had at hand, saw that his accounts were in order, and took his own life—with the same proud calmness that he would have shown if he had been accepting a gift of thanks from the emperor.

"My duty is to act the part assigned to me well." That was the rule by which the Stoics lived and Seneca died. The man who said it first was Epictetus, a teacher of the emperor Trajan and a friend of the emperor Hadrian. When he had first come to Italy from Phrygia, he had been one of a boatload of slaves. He was sold to a rich freedman in the court of Nero. He was not a good buy, for he was young and crippled, but his new master thought that he might make something of him. He seemed bright and, though he bore his troubles patiently, he carried himself with pride.

Epictetus was sent to school, and there he learned about the philosophy of the Stoics. The part of a slave and a cripple was not an easy one to play without complaining. But Epictetus grew in courage and wisdom, until his master was so impressed that he set him free. Then Epictetus opened his own school, and some of the greatest men in Rome came to him as humble pupils.

Fate assigned a very different part to another Roman Stoic, Marcus Aurelius. No one could set him free, for he was an emperor. He was one of the two chosen by Hadrian from among all the eager generals and statesmen. It seemed to Hadrian that young Marcus had spent his life preparing to take on the most difficult job in the world—ruling Rome. As a child, he had trained himself so strictly that his mother had had a difficult time persuading him to sleep on a bed of sheepskins instead of the bare ground. A few years later, he began to study the teachings of Epictetus. When Hadrian first met him, Marcus was still a boy, but already he had won a name for seriousness and bravery. Hadrian was certain that this boy could grow up to be the wise commander that the troubled Romans needed. So he chose as his own heir a gentle, elderly statesman, Antoninus Pius, and asked him to adopt Marcus Aurelius as his son.

For the first time, Rome was ruled by men whose one interest was the good of all of the people. Old Antoninus was kind and just. In the twenty-three years of his reign, from 138 to 161, he taught the Romans to forget the fears which they had learned in the time of Nero and Domitian. True to his promise to Hadrian, he made young Marcus his junior partner, a strong right arm to guard his justice.

COMMODUS DELIGHTED IN FIGHTING IN THE ARENA, BUT HE ALWAYS HAD TO WIN.

THE BARBARIANS ATTACK

When Antoninus died, Marcus Aurelius had become the man of wisdom that Hadrian had hoped he would be. He accepted the responsibilities of the empire with all the nobility and courage of his philosophy. In his little book, *Meditations,* he wrote the command which he gave to himself each day: "Every moment think steadily, as a Roman and a man."

Rome needed a ruler with such strength, for in 167, the sixth year of Marcus' reign, the two centuries of the great Peace of Rome came sharply to an end. Barbaric German tribes broke through the border fortifications and poured down into Italy. They were driven back, but new wars broke out in the north. Then attacks along the eastern frontier showed up the weakness of the defenses which Hadrian had labored to make strong. The attackers were more powerful than they had been before, and when one of their armies was beaten, another turned up somewhere else along the frontier.

For the rest of his life, Marcus Aurelius hurried from the Danube country to Asia and back, fighting to hold the line that meant the difference between peace and the end of the empire. In 180, he died in Vienna, still on campaign.

His son, Commodus, whom Marcus left to rule Rome, was a braggart with a coward's cruelty. Proud of his strength, he fought in the arenas with the gladiators. His opponents were carefully chosen, and somehow they were never the best fighters. But after he had been emperor for a year or so, Commodus could boast that he had killed thousands, using (he always said) his left hand only. This noisy hero ran through all the money in the treasury, earned the hatred of his people, and finally, in A.D. 192, was assassinated. He was strangled by his wrestling teacher at the order of the captain of the Praetorian Guard.

Meanwhile, the borders were crumbling. The Romans went on spending their money and, like their late emperor, they gloried in their strength—a strength they no longer possessed.

The End of the City

A.D. 192-A.D. 476

On Rome's first day, Romulus took a bronze plow and drew a magic circle around seven of the hills that stood beside the River Tiber. The magic of the circle was protection against the evils outside. More important, it bound together the people who were inside, making one city where there had been six towns.

Seven hundred years later, Augustus drew another magic circle, this time around all the Mediterranean world. It kept out barbarian and Asian invaders and held together millions of people, making one empire where there had been dozens of races and nations. So long as the circle had its magic power, Rome would exist.

But there was no magic in the circles themselves. The real magic had been in Romulus himself, a chief who was strong and wise enough to build a city. There had been magic, too, in Augus-

DIOCLETIAN'S PALACE AT SPALATO WAS A LANDMARK OF LATE IMPERIAL ROME. AT RIGHT ARE FOUR HIGH ROMAN OFFICIALS.

tus, whose wisdom had brought order and peace to an empire. Without such men, the circles were powerless. Invaders and conquerors could break through them. The people and countries they held together would fall apart. And that was what happened to Rome after the death of Marcus Aurelius.

TOO MANY CAESARS

It did not happen all at once. There was still an empire and there were emperors who tried to rule it—too many, in fact. When Commodus was murdered, four would-be rulers, each with a Roman army behind him, fought over the throne. The winner, Septimus Severus, the commander of the Danube troops, held it for eighteen years. When he was about to die, he gave his two sons a piece of advice about ruling Rome: "Stick together, pay the soldiers, and forget the rest."

But his sons did not stick together. When Septimus was dead, each of them tried to be the emperor. Caracalla, the elder of the two, settled the dispute by murdering his brother. Then he remembered his father's words and set out to grab as much money as he could for his soldiers and, of course, for himself. Years later, he was remembered as the emperor who had the wisdom and generosity to grant the rights of Roman citizenship to all the freemen of the empire. It was an important step in the development of Rome, but at the time, many people said it was only Caracalla's way to add to the number of Romans who paid taxes to him. If he meant it as an act of generosity, it was his first and last. Afterwards, he gave the citizens of Rome five years of the kind of rule that had made Nero and Caligula famous. The captain of the Praetorian Guard again saw his duty, and Caracalla was murdered. Then the armies took over the business of picking a new emperor.

Some of these soldier-emperors scarcely had time to sit down on the throne before they were pushed off again by a rival or by their own mutinous troops. In seventy years, more than seventy-five men claimed the title *Augustus* and the imperial power that went with it. In one year alone, six emperors were proclaimed, enthroned, and murdered by their troops.

The circle that held the empire was splintered. Civil wars destroyed all order inside it. Government in the capital was a muddle of confused clerks and officials who did not know from one day to the next which emperor they were working for. When the treasury ran out of money, copper coins had to be made instead of silver ones. That sent prices up until people could no longer afford to pay them. Then business stopped; citizens and government alike faced ruin.

TROUBLE IN THE PROVINCES

In the provinces, it was even worse. Laws were openly disobeyed. Robbery and murder went unpunished. Along the splendid Roman roads, bands of thieves preyed on travelers and the merchants' caravans.

When the legions left the frontiers to fight in the battles for the throne, wave after wave of barbaric invaders rushed through the weak spots along the borders. In Britain, Hadrian's wall was pierced, then overwhelmed. Raiders from the Asian kingdoms made frequent attacks along the eastern frontier, weakening defenses that were already crumbling. There was no power in Augustus' circle now. And, when the city of Rome began to build a fortified wall for its own defense, fear and unrest in the provinces turned into panic.

In Syria, the beautiful, dark-haired Queen Zenobia of Palmyra set up an independent kingdom of her own. Proclaiming herself the descendant of Cleopatra, she led a revolt against the empire. All of Egypt and half of Asia Minor went with her, and it was three years before the legionaries arrived to disperse her troops. Then Palmyra was burned to the ground and Zenobia, bound in chains of gold, was led away to Rome. But her defiance had set an example, and other revolts sprang up as local leaders realized that they no longer looked to Rome for protection. No longer could they count on the power of the emperor. Often they could not be sure who he was.

Fear and poverty haunted the cities. Trade fell off and farmers began to leave their fields unplanted. The plague broke out again; for fifteen years it raged across the empire. Earthquakes destroyed many of the Asian towns. And still the parade of emperors and would-be emperors went on in Rome.

DIOCLETIAN RESTORES ORDER

Then, in A.D. 284, it stopped. A general named Diocletian, who seemed no different from all the others, refused to be pushed aside. The Romans were startled, for Diocletian was no one's favorite among the four generals who had their eyes on the throne that year. But he overcame all of his rivals, and the Romans looked him over again. Could he succeed where so many others had failed? With a keen mind and an iron fist, Diocletian held his throne for twenty years. In that time, he ran his own circle of power around the empire, and gave it the strength to last for eighty years more. To many Romans, however, it seemed more like a prison wall. Diocletian's soldiers were posted everywhere, not just on the frontiers. Bakers and food merchants had to feed them without being paid for it. Shipowners transported them for nothing. Taxes went higher and higher, and the emperor made the rich men in town responsible for collecting them. They could get the money or grain from their neighbors, or pay all of it themselves, or go to prison. Before long, the Romans discovered that making money was not worth while, because they got to keep so little of it. But when they tried to close their businesses or to give up their farms, Diocletian passed a law that forbade them to do it. Their sons, too, were forced by law to keep the family businesses going. Soldiers' sons had no choice but to go into the army. And farm workers were not allowed to move to another farm, much less to another sort of job. So they went on working, not for themselves but for the empire and the emperor. The price for peace and order was high, and the Romans paid it with their freedom as well as with their money.

Yet many citizens did not mind the new system. The empire had taken care of them for so long that they could not imagine what it would be like to take care of themselves. They needed a *pater familias* in Rome. The idea of losing some of their freedom—even the right to choose their own jobs—did not frighten them nearly as much as the idea of not being looked after. And then there were the millions of freemen who had once been slaves. Slavery had taught them to obey a master and not to complain. Given their freedom, they still took the good or the bad that came their way without complaining, and they felt easier when someone told them what to do.

Diocletian was more than ready to give the orders. He made himself *pater familias,* master, and a god. Though his mother had been a slave and he had had to work his way through the rough ranks of the legions, he proclaimed himself a god-king. Dressed in the pearl-encrusted crown and silken robes of an Oriental monarch, he commanded the citizens of the empire to call him *Jovius,* the child of Jupiter, and *Dominus,* sacred lord. Of course, he was *Augustus* too.

He was willing to share his power, however. Closing the frontiers to invaders was more work than one commander could do, so he took charge of the eastern borders himself and gave the job of holding the west to his trusted officer, Maximian. He also gave him the name *Augustus* and all the honors of an emperor.

Two emperors—and two empires? Not yet, but when Diocletian made his plan, he drew a line down the center of the Roman world. In a hundred years, that line became a crack. Then it broke open, and no emperor or magic could put it together again.

But for twenty-one years, Diocletian held the empire in one piece with the strength of his troops and his laws. Then, satisfied with his work and realizing that he was growing old, he resigned and persuaded Maximian to do the same. This was a special kind of triumph, because Diocletian gave up his office and his crown in the same way that he had won them: by his own will and by his own power. Before he retired, he named the men who were to take over his government. But within two years there were six eager emperors fighting over the throne. When any of them asked Diocletian's help, he refused to give it. Perhaps he felt as Alexander did when he was asked who should rule his empire after he was gone. Alexander had replied, "It must go to the strongest."

Diocletian's empire went at last to Constantine, a man who said he had no strength in himself at all. The power which brought him victory, he said, was the power of his god, the god of the Christians. On the night before his greatest battle, he had seen in the sky a glowing cross and the words, *In hoc signo vinces*—"By this sign you will conquer." This, he said, was God's way of telling him that he had been chosen to rule Rome. He did not have to call himself a god in order to be the emperor, and the people did not have to worship him. But, in obeying him, they also obeyed God, because God had selected him to govern them.

CONSTANTINE THE CHRISTIAN

So now the Christian God, whom so many emperors had feared as a danger to their own power, became the defender of emperors. Many of the Romans, whether they were Christians or not, liked the idea. It had always been hard to believe that a rough soldier was a god just because he had defeated all the other soldiers who wanted to be emperor. It was easier to believe that a soldier had been chosen to rule by a god and had been given the power and wisdom to do it. For the next 1,400 years or more, the kings of Europe would claim their thrones by this same "divine right."

Although Constantine was a Christian, he did not try to stamp out the other religions in the empire, nor did he pass laws against them. He did decree that there would be two capital cities of Rome—the Italian one of Romulus and Caesar, and a new eastern one of his own. In the new city his churches would not be surrounded by old pagan temples.

The place he chose for the new Rome was Byzantium, the ancient Greek stronghold on the Hellespont. The Greek settlers had been told to build there by the Oracle, the priestess who spoke with the wisdom of the gods, and it was wise advice. Byzantium stood at the spot where the land route between Asia and the Danube jumps across the channel between the Black Sea and the Mediterranean—truly a crossroads of the world. The hilly little peninsula, bound by water on three sides, was a superb natural fortress and had a fine harbor. It was beautiful as well. Constantine

AT BYZANTIUM, CONSTANTINE BUILT THE NEW ROME.

shipped his architects and builders to the old town, and they went to work.

Four years later, in the year 330, the New Rome was ready. The first visitors were amazed to find a dozen palaces rising on the hills, and churches, triumphal arches, huge Roman baths, and a stately arena, the Hippodrome. Wherever the visitors went, along the streets or in the shining new buildings, they came upon treasures of art which had been collected from every corner of the ancient world. Each was a reminder of the cities and nations that made up Constantine's empire and whose men filled the ranks of his legions. For he had built a capital to match the empire—a city of the world. And no one called it New Rome; everyone called it Constantinople, the city of Constantine.

The other capital, the old Rome, began to seem a little old-fashioned. It was quieter, too. No triumphal processions filled its streets with cheering throngs, and the color and excitement of the court were gone. The Senate still met, but it was little more than a city council. Italy itself was just another province now, and an Italian was no more important than a man from any other part of the empire. Some Romans began to wonder if perhaps two empires, with Rome as the only capital of one of them, might not be a good idea.

Constantine, however, was determined that there would be only one empire. It was his dream that Christianity would hold together the people of his Roman world and then bring the men of all parts of the earth into one fellowship. While the second part of his dream came close to coming true, the first did not.

When Constantine died, his sons, like the sons of many emperors, fought over his throne. The line which Diocletian had drawn along the middle of the empire cracked open. There were two empires, and only once did a strong emperor, Theodosius I, manage to put the two pieces together. Even then, it lasted for only three years. When Theodosius died in 395, his sons divided it between them.

Meanwhile, the Roman world was furiously attacked from every side. A new Asian power battered at the eastern frontier, and barbarians from as far north as Denmark and Sweden hacked at the borders in Britain, Gaul, and Spain.

Constantinople, halfway between the Danube and Euphrates fronts, had been the natural headquarters for military operations when the empire was whole. Now, when the circle of defense which centered on the eastern capital was drawn tight for strength, Rome was left outside. There was a Roman empire still, but the city which had built it was no longer a part of it.

In the West, the pieces of the old empire fell apart as soon as the invaders touched them. In A.D. 406, the Rhine defenses collapsed. Britain had already been lost. Gaul and Spain went next, then North Africa. In 410, a horde of Goths, under the fierce chief Alaric, captured the city of Rome. The Goths did not stay, but the men who called themselves the emperors of Rome could no longer pretend to have the power to rule it, and after 476, there were no emperors at all.

CONSTANTINE TRIED TO PRESERVE THE EMPIRE, BUT HIS TWO SONS DIVIDED IT.

"THE ROMANS CAME THIS WAY"

In 753 B.C., Romulus had seen a sign of twelve eagles, a promise from the gods that his new city would last for 1,200 years. It was only a story, of course. But in A.D. 476, when the last of the emperors disappeared from Rome, the city was 1,229 years old. There were some people who wondered if Rome had not already outlived its destiny and was fated soon to die.

Many of the Romans seemed almost not to care. They were worn out, like the fields of Italy which had been planted for too many years and no longer had the strength to grow healthy crops. No new armies came from the hills and plains to fight under Mars, the war god. Mars himself was dead. His temples still stood, but Rome was becoming a Christian city. Jupiter and Juno and Apollo were dead, too, and the ancient world died with them. When Rome became important again, it was as the first city of the new religion, a capital in the modern world.

The eastern empire became a part of that modern world. For a thousand years it held together, a monument to the power and practical sense of Roman conquerors. The ideas of the ancient world lived on, too, in the minds of the men who lived in the western world which Greece and Rome had begun.

From Constantinople a man could look across the Hellespont to Troy. There, the storytellers said, the Greeks had fought their first great battle. There Alexander the Great had found his hero Achilles. There the Trojan prince Aeneas had begun the journey that led to Rome. A man who stood on a hill in Constantinople stood in the old world and the new at the same time. In both worlds, he saw the unmistakable marks that said, "The Romans came this way." And, like the ancients, he could say about Rome, "This is the city which, sprung from humble beginnings, has stretched to either pole, and from one small place has extended her power wherever the sun gives its light."

IMPORTANT DATES AND EVENTS

42 B.C. Octavius, Antony and Lepidus form the Second Triumvirate, and destroy Cassius and Brutus at battle of Philippi.

41-31 B.C. Rivalry between Octavius and Antony develops into war.

31 B.C. Fleet of Antony and Cleopatra beaten by Octavius at the battle of Actium.

30 B.C. Antony and Cleopatra kill themselves; Octavius becomes Augustus.

29 B.C.-A.D. 14 Reign of Augustus; the Empire at peace; the arts and culture flourish.

A.D. 14-117 A series of emperors rules Rome.

A.D. 64 Fire devastates Rome; Nero blames it on Christians.

A.D. 68 Nero, last of Caesar family, commits suicide to avoid assassination at the hands of his guards.

A.D. 79 Eruption of Vesuvius buries town of Pompeii under lava.

A.D. 106 Legions under Emperor Trajan push the borders of the Empire beyond the Danube River.

A.D. 117-138 Reign of Hadrian; trade flourishes; walls built on the borders to stop barbarians.

IN ROMAN HISTORY, 42 B.C.-A.D. 476

A.D. 138-180 Hadrian's successors, Antoninus and Marcus Aurelius, govern the Empire.

A.D. 167 Barbarians break through the border defenses into Italy and are beaten back with difficulty.

A.D. 192-284 Chaos in the Empire; the borders are breached; revolts in the provinces; trade falls off; famine and plague in the cities.

A.D. 284-305 Diocletian restores order by making the Empire an armed camp ruled by the legions.

A.D. 324 Constantine, a Christian, becomes Emperor.

A.D. 326 Constantine begins to build a new capital for the Empire at Byzantium on the Hellespont.

A.D. 395 At death of Theodosius, his two sons divide the Empire between them; it is never reunited.

A.D. 406 The Rhine defenses collapse before waves of barbarian invaders; Gaul is overrun.

A.D. 410 Visigoths under Alaric capture and sack the city of Rome.

A.D. 476 Emperor Romulus deposed by barbarians, bringing the Roman Empire in the West to an end; Caesar's heirs still rule the East.

INDEX

PICTURE CREDITS

VOLUME 3

Inside front cover and facing page, clockwise from top left: Head of Hermes, Rome, terra cotta, 6th century B.C., Villa Giulia Museum, Rome; two wrestlers, Etruscan, bronze, 4th-3rd centuries B.C., Walters Art Gallery, Baltimore; fresco, Etruscan, 6th century B.C., National Museum, Tarquinia; Maenad, Etruscan, terra cotta, 6th century B.C., Villa Giulia Museum, Rome; tripod, Etruscan (detail), bronze, 540-530 B.C., Staatliche Antikensammlungen, Munich; head of a man, Rome, marble, 240 A.D., Museo Nuovo Capitolino, German Archeological Institute, Rome; necklace, Etruscan, silver, 6th century B.C., Louvre, Paris; head of a woman, Rome, marble, Cincinnati Art Museum; satyr dancing, Etruscan, terra cotta, 5th century B.C., Villa Giulia Museum, Rome; funerary urn, Etruscan, National Museum, Tarquinia; Emperors Claudius and Germanicus with their wives, onyx cameo, 1st century B.C., Kunsthistorisches Museum, Vienna; Etruscan urn, terra cotta, 7th century B.C., Staatliche Museen, Berlin; Emperor Philip the Arabian, Rome, silver, 244 A.D., Boston Museum of Fine Arts.

Inside back cover and facing page, clockwise from top left: frieze of "Sacrifice of Souvetaurilia," Rome, Louvre, Paris (Alinari); Roman actor, marble, 45-64 A.D., Ny Carlsberg Glyptotek, Copenhagen; lion, Etruscan, gold, 5th century B.C., Celle Museum, Rome; Colosseum, Rome, constructed 70-82 A.D., Fototeca Unione, Rome; house of the Nymphaeum, 350-400 A.D., Ostia; dying Adonis, Rome, terra cotta, 1st century B.C., Vatican Museum, Rome; Roman eagle, onyx cameo, 1st century B.C., Kunsthistoriches Museum, Vienna; naumachia, Rome, National Museum, Naples; lion, Etruscan, gold, 5th century B.C., Celle Museum, Rome.

Other pages: 180 bird, Etruscan, fresco, 6th century B.C., tomb of the Augurs, Tarquinia; **186** "La lupa dei Campidoglio," Etruscan Art, 5th century B.C., Palace of the Conservators, Rome; **197** mask, Carthage, polychromed glass, 2nd century B.C., Alaoui Museum, Tunis; **204** Scipio, Musée du Capitole, Rome; **210** gladiator's helmet, Rome, bronze, Imperial period, Louvre, Paris; **217** Roman eagle, stone, Imperial period, Buonarotti Gallery, Florence; **223** (top) Pompey, after a sculpture in National Museum, Naples; **228** Augustus Caesar, Rome, marble, 44 A.D., Arles Museum; **234** Augustus Caesar, Rome, stone, Imperial period, Louvre, Paris; **240-241** Roman coins, bronze, Imperial period, private collection; **247** Emperor Hadrian, Rome, marble, 2nd century A.D., British Museum, London; **261** "The Tetrarchs," Rome, porphyry, 4th century A.D., St. Mark's, Venice; **265** Emperor Constantine, Eastern Empire, bronze, 4th century A.D., National Museum, Belgrade.